The Healing Power of God's Love

My Journey

Author: William (Bill) Billard

Table of Contents

My Journey

I press forward to overcome a life of pain and embrace miracles.

Chapter 10 Are you all right, do I need to call an ambulance?

Chapter 11 Conclusion, God's plan for my life, a search for meaning out of chaos

Authors note

I am writing this book for you. I am an aging senior who has walked an unusual path through life. It is a meandering path of wildly differing motivations, some creative, some adventurous, some self-destructive, some redeeming.

I am writing this book from two perspectives.

One is the learned personal experience wisdom and knowledge gained from those divergent paths. The other perspective is the collective experience and wisdom of many voices of the past, as well as voices of wisdom in our contemporary age.

I am writing this book so you may have an opportunity to broaden your perspective about the management of your personal health and wellbeing. I am not a guru. I am not writing this book to create a following.

I am writing it for you to learn to strengthen your personal relationship with your Creator. Through that strengthened relationship, you will learn to trust God to do His part in providing divine health and healing.

He is the only one who is capable of being your wise advisor. He is the only one who truly knows you as well as you know yourself. The real truth is He knows you far better than you know yourself.

I am writing this Journey from the perspective of my personal experience. My greatest hope is for you to read this book and learn from the combination of perspectives.

Finally, in those adaptations you make, I pray for healing for your broken places, whether they be physical, emotional, spiritual or personal knowledge.

Introduction

Consider the most memorable creative moment of your life. Maybe that moment was when you accomplished the most challenging task of your work life. Maybe if you are a parent, it was the moment you held your child in your arms for the first time. Maybe your dearest memory was as a child when you created something special to give to your mom or dad as a gift at Christmas.

I invite you stop reading for a moment and remember your most personal creative moment.....

When you were reliving the experience, what did you feel? Did you feel the joy of seeing your creation finished and ready for others to appreciate? Did they enjoy the fruit of your creativity? Did you feel the appreciation of their praise of your finished work?

More importantly, did you feel a special love within you for what you created? Where you thrilled when you saw your simple idea taking shape as the result of your labor?

If you were in touch with any or all of the emotions I have just described, will you agree those emotionally packed memories are a real and dear part of your legacy of personal heritage? They are a part of your unique identity.

Where you excited about the process of revelation you experienced as you grew your idea from a simple thought to a complete perfect picture in your mind? I encourage you to be in touch with the feeling of love, a genuine appreciation, which is the compelling desire for creative expression.

Creativity does not just happen by chance. It is a carefully thought out process beginning with inspiration.

Encouragement sparks inspiration to bloom into the intense desire to take action. Persistent work fuels the desire into a flaming creative force, a passion for your creation. Are you in touch with your creativity in a new way?

Now imagine as best as you can the intense love you would experience if you were able to create hundreds or even billions of your best creative ideas. Imagine each one being unique and different. Now imagine each of your creations ALIVE..... Are you breathless?

Imagine God speaking to you at this moment:

""Here beloved, I give you my most cherished creation. Here is your unique body, mind, and spirit. I give it to you freely in an open palm. I give it to you with no expectations of perfection, only the hope of a loving father that you will come to love My gift, your life.

I hope you noticed how finely I crafted every detail to please you. I hope you saw how well it fits your particular unique expressions, emotions, and experiences.

I am still in the process of creating you from moment to moment. You are never the same as you used to be.

I want you to accept my gift with a humble appreciation of me your creator. You're a great and unique treasure. Take this moment and notice. Now begin to realize how much I love you?"

By the way, do not fret if your body is not performing as flawlessly as it once did. I planned for your season of poor performance as well. I created within every cell of your body unique repair abilities.

These special abilities can add extra years of abundant life for you. They can return youthful bounce to your step. They can be the source of the greatest joy you have ever experienced. Notice I said "can" not "will"?

Remember in all creative and re-creative process there has first to be an inspiration. I am the source of all inspiration. I have picked a servant to craft this book for you. Allow it to become a part of your source of inspiration for my healing in your life.

You are the most useful in my plan for your life when your body is whole, healthy, and growing the way I intended. Ask me for my help, and I will begin the process of your healing. I will provide a dear friend for you. I will speak perfect words of peace and hope to you through your friend.

Those words will provide the spark of encouragement you need to begin your healing journey. You will know I am their source because they will confirm the truth I have already spoken into your heart.

Learn to trust me in the process. I will provide you with the fuel of intense desire to be whole and healed. Finally, I will craft in you a new and perfect heart of love for me. A special heart filled with joy as you lovingly fulfill my particular and unique plan for you. May these pages bless you as you read them in the same intense, joyous way they have blessed my servant as he crafted them.""

You're Loving Father,

Creator of All

Why Am I still Here Lord?

I awaken many mornings with this thought capturing the sharp focus of my attention. During my teenage years when the question began to awaken me, I would feel intense sadness in the absence of answers to the dilemma of my continuing life.

Those mornings my thoughts would run a litany of reasons why my life should have already come to an end. Why didn't you take me when I fell through the big hole in the floor and landed in our basement when I was three years old. Why didn't you take me when I fell out of a tree and broke my arm when I was twelve, or later that year when I was in the hospital with diphtheria?

Those years, suffering and pain coupled with confusion and delusion were my normal daily perception. However, even in those days of continual despair, there were many brief moments when I could disengage my focus from the pain and take delight in the intense images of my imagination as I soared off in some heavenly quest to discover something new about the mystery and majesty of Gods massively amazing creation.

I could go for that interlude, be it a few brief minutes or an hour, and connect with an intense desire for a future life of soaring effortlessly above and beyond any obstacle preventing me from satisfying my intense curiosity.

Then when the next moment of reality crashed upon me, I was at least capable of enduring the next moment of pain as I experienced the hostile nature of this world. Still in the innermost part of my being I knew. This world is not where I belong. This pain is not what I want to endure for much longer.

Now a full lifetime later, I am still here. The painful moments still come to this accident prone body whose mind still daydreams of Heavenly places instead of focusing on the task of the moment.

Yes, I still long for the day when I can soar through the heavens breathlessly filling my insatiable curiosity. Now, however, I fill many of these life moments experiencing intense joy in the simple pleasures of living life as it presents itself.

Often, my moment is a quiet one asking God a different "why am I still here?" question. I simply say, Lord what do you have for me to do today that demonstrates your love?

When He shows me my task, I jump in boldly and labor through with patient kindness for the next precious person He has skillfully arranged for me to meet and share transparent moments of loving and honoring our Creator.

Someday, sooner than later in my now "old man's perspective." I will come to that time when I will forever soar in the heavens. Now I know. However, I want to spend many humbly grateful days laying flat on my face before the Throne worshiping my King of Kings and Lord of Lords.

Until that day, I will be content with the next adventure laid out before me in this amazing life here on this earth. I invite you to come along with me through the journey that transformed me from despair to intense loving joy.

My Journey

I press forward to overcome a life of pain and embrace miracles.

Chapter 1

Who do you want to live with Daddy or me?

I created you to have a growing personal relationship with me

""Before I began the task of creating You, I began the tasks of creating everything else as well. I am not a creator who merely hurled out the vastness of the entire universe at the beginning of time in one "Big Bang" and finished it all. I do not just sit back and watch as my perfect plan turns from perfect to chaos.

No, that is not who I am. I am the infinitely aware creating force existing and aware of every detail of my creating process every moment; I am creating! Nothing is beyond my awareness. I am not the Creator, I am the Creating Presence, and I am in loving, patient control of it all.

My process of creating is simple. Create, observe, learn, and adapt my creation. To the eye of the casual observer, what I produce may seem random and chaotic. To my carefully discerning eye of ageless perspective, my creation is always fresh, new and continually expanding in planned growth.

Simply stated, I only operate from one single orientation. I enhance and grow all things. Those who carefully observe this constant phenomenon can identify its subtle characteristics. They define those fruitful characteristics as, love, joy, harmony, peace, patience, self-control, and perseverance. Everything I create and maintain is inseparable from those elements.

There is one part of my creation, a mere speck in my creative eye that holds a special place in my attention.

I created you, and every member of Mankind to become co-creator with me. I create each one of you individually to perform a small portion of my great task of creation. Some plant, some harvest, some use the rewards of the crop to nurture and prepare the next generation.

All learn, create, observe their creation, adapt, and finally contribute their individual knowledge, their wisdom, to strengthen the collective knowledge of humanity. I have implanted this creative process in you. You are a precious part of my co-creating plan. I desire to see you grow as much as you possibly can.""

I do not know of any other question that could have been asked of me that had as much of an instant awakening to reality as my Mom's words. I was four years old. I can still clearly remember the scene.

It was a winter morning in 1950. We were living in the home of my birth on Staten Island, New York. The three of us kids gathered with mom around the open door of the kitchen oven trying to get warm.

Before that morning, I had no recall of specific events. I would assume that my earlier developmental years were "normal." Obviously, however, from Mom's question, our home was not the predictable place I perceived it to be.

We stayed together as a family for many more years, but from then on I was always aware of the steadily escalating family conflict as it became the norm for the rest of my childhood.

I was third in the birth order with an 18 month older sister and a five year older brother.

In light of what I now know about fetal learning, I have no doubt there was plenty of cause for fear and anxiety in our home. A major piece of it was the ending of World War II and return home of my Dad.

I have little doubt my older sibs early childhood noisiness was a major factor in my entrenched coping habit of blocking out and therefore ignoring anything I did not want to hear. At four years old I became an expert in the art of denial.

My dad returned home from duty in England with a full load of war terrors and fears unresolved. He was hospitalized, and treated under VA psychiatric care for an untold number of years.

The fact of his VA care was the most closely held of our family secrets because no one would want to associate with a man "crazy" enough to need to see a psychiatrist.

Despite his ongoing treatment, Dad was functional. He did his best to be a consistent above average provider for our family. Dad was self-absorbed, driven to succeed, and intelligent but unschooled past the 8th grade.

At 14, He was forced to quit school, and become the sole provider for his Mom and his four younger siblings, the product of a broken home.

Resentment and regret of that early adult responsibility riveted the focus of his attention on his past. He transferred that resentment to the crisis of the moment in our daily lives. If only we would just shape up and comply with his demands, we could live in peace.

His best attempts to bring about the order he desperately desired became lost or ignored by us because of the intensity of his anger. We shut him out of our thoughts rather than just simply comply with his persistent demands.

To be fair, there were no post-traumatic stress disorder or 12 step recovery therapies in place in society in the early fifties to help him openly look at ways to deal with his past life wounds much less his war-related horrors.

He was expected instead to take his place as a part of a male dominated, legalistic, authority based social norm. There was no tolerance allowed for anything but male dominance. My Dad just did not know any other point of view.

He lived the life he had learned and had no insight in how to develop healthier coping skills or healthy loving family relationships.

My first recollection of Spiritual life was singing "Jesus loves me" in Episcopal nursery vacation bible school. I didn't know who Jesus was, but I knew that my Grandpa was with Him in heaven. Grandpa Jewels (My step-grandfather) died of a heart attack earlier that same year.

We loved the smiling, cheerful attention Grandpa gave us kids when he would come to our home and visit every Saturday night.

My second spiritual awakening memory was when we started attending the big beautiful Presbyterian cathedral. I can remember being awed by its beauty as I gazed at the beautiful stained glass windows.

I didn't even mind that I had to sit through the service because I was fascinated by the scenes in the stained glass the quiet reverence of the service and the enormous sound of the huge pipe organ in the balcony. I could easily imagine that this was what heaven would be like where Grandpa was.

Life changed radically over the course of the next three years. Our family grew with the addition of two more sisters. My dad was battling the crippling effects of rheumatoid arthritis.

He was advised by his doctors to move to a warmer dryer climate. So in 1953, He sold our home and moved the entire family to Dallas Texas to start a new and different life.

We shifted lifestyle as a family of 7 living in a three bedroom home and became a family of 7 stuffed into in a 30 x 8-foot house trailer with no bathroom.

There were three small rooms and barely enough floor space for our folding chairs as we sat and ate around the hidden pull out leaf dining table in the living room. It took less than a year for the strain of that cramped life to take a significant toll on our family.

The first event was the rebellion of my then 12-year-old brother Kenneth. He missed Staten Island and wanted to return to his real home. He ran away, broke into a church, and wound up a becoming juvenile burglary offender at that early age.

That first experience of criminal behavior and a rebellious spirit plagued my brother for the rest of his life. Kenneth's crime was the second most carefully held family secret and the largest source of family shame and discord from that time on.

At age 9, I was learning from Kenneth's negative example what I did not want to become when I grew older. I did not want to become a criminal like Kenneth, and I also did not want to be the angry, argumentative resentful person I continually witnessed in my Dad.

By age 12, I made a vow to myself to not have my kids grow up in the kind of oppression or shame and guilt I was experiencing.

I spent my adolescent years desiring to show my Dad that he had a son who could make him proud and happy. I strived to be that son, but whatever best efforts I put forth, they were never good enough to please him.

My failures to satisfy him added layer upon layer of punishment, guilt, and shame. Self-blame was the only logical conclusion I could make about my failures. I just must not be good enough or maybe worse, not good at all.

My quandary of hopelessness became my dominant pattern of thought from those terrible years until much later in my adult life. Defeat and chronic depression were my constant companions.

Our life as a family struggled on, but the toll of discord and continual strife led to the breakup and divorce of my parents shortly after I turned 14.

Fortunately for me, I did not have to repeat my father's plight and assume the role of provider as the oldest male still living at home. My mom worked, and we made ends meet with her limited income, child support, and a lot less stress in the family.

During the first years in Dallas, We changed faith and began attending a small Methodist church. It was a bright spot of my life in the midst of all the strife at home.

I lived in defeated meekness yearning to be loved. "Blessed are the meek" I knew in my heart that Beatitude perfectly described my life. The pain of others became my own. I cared deeply about their suffering because I knew it so well and longed to be able to ease theirs as well as my own.

I endured the dominating selfish behavior of the bullies at school and the bully at home. I knew, without a doubt, bullying cruelty was not how God wanted us to behave. I gave my heart to Jesus at the age of 11.

After our family breakup, we went to church at wherever church my Mom's boyfriend of the moment attended. I became a Baptist, then a Seventh Day Adventist.

Expectations of my behavior also changed dramatically, and I quickly lost sight of the quiet, loving reverence of my past worship experiences.

My daily life became immersed in behavioral rules and strict compliance to religious authority.

As a Seventh Day Adventist, I learned a lot of Bible history and prophecy, and everything I could about Christ's return in the Second Advent.

I was certain Jesus would return soon, and take us all home with him. If only I could become good enough to be included in the elect. In the beginning, my core self-loathing thought pattern morphed into a new dynamic of shame and guilt. I earnestly strived to live a pure life and be accepted, but strict, rigid compliance was foreign to my undisciplined mind.

What I did not learn was that I could have a personal relationship with my Lord and Savior Jesus Christ. Yes, I strived to learn and accept it all the doctrines, but what I did not know was that all those rules without the emphasis on personal relationship with God would ultimately lead me to rebellion.

I spent my senior year of High School living away from home in a Seventh Day Adventist Academy and college close to Dallas.

I worked my first real job every morning and went to school in the afternoon. At 16, I was self-supporting and independent from my family.

The beginning of a temporary counterpoint to my defeated perception of self-worth began emerging. My new self could succeed. This young man was scholastically bright and worthy of respect by my peers and teachers. I looked forward to attending college there the next year and felt the stirrings of a call to pursue a medical career.

However, fate stepped in, and I returned home to my family. My Mom broke off her engagement with Mac, the Seventh Day Adventist man who was an active, loving mentor and encouragement to me.

I was needed at home to share the task of helping support our family, and I quickly found a job as an orderly in the emergency room of Parkland Hospital.

My broken-hearted mom made a life-changing decision to give up on God and a life of faith. She openly rebelled against the "hypocrites" in the church who rejected her because of her country and western dancing nightclub lifestyle and those who influenced the destruction of her relationship with Mac. She became bitter dancing and resentful, blaming everyone for the end of her hopes and dreams with Mac.

She never about the idea of accepting the truth of her responsibility to live a life of prayer, peace and hope and joy in relationship with God. She too was forced by "religion" to focus on her inability to be good enough in "their" eyes.

For the rest of her life, she never resolved her wounds of her heart. Never again would she listen to any conversation or truth about God's love. Her continuing bitter commentary about religion and religious hypocrites set the stage for my 30 year period of rebellion during adult life.

One year later, just after my 18th birthday, I joined the Navy. The year was 1964, and the Viet Nam war was escalating. I had just registered for the draft and knew my induction into the Army was imminent. Or, If I chose wisely, I could escape becoming a casualty of direct fire by joining the Navy. I chose the safer path.

Within four years of naval service, I was married and had started my family. I still carried all the unresolved baggage of my personal identity issues from childhood and now faced in the role of being the provider for my household.

My confidence in self once again began to crumble as I tried to cope unsuccessfully with the relational and physical challenges of married life.

Self-doubt and self-loathing quickly replaced the outer directed mask of being the confident military leader/achiever that hallmarked my first four years of service.

The first thing to disintegrate was my spiritual life. I was required to convert to the Latter Day Saint religion as a condition of marriage to my Mormon fiance.

I converted, and soon afterward found plenty of doctrine and legalism to help me decide that my overseas navy liberty time was much better spent having fun with my shipboard buddies in the bars of the nearest port of call.

At age 24, I discovered the "Counterculture new age philosophy." Yes, while I was still in the Navy, I became a closet "short haired Hippy."

I agreed completely with the notion of mass cultural rebellion. Those of us who were "enlightened" against the old norms of male dominated authority based society had a vision of a better future.

The establishment had to go! War had to end! Pragmatic and reactionary attitudes must end before society could move forward into the new dawning age of truth, maturity, and equality.

I believed every word of it and wrapped my identity into actively promoting the radical social change. The "New Age" held up the hope and promise that we "the aware, hip generation" could alter the world with our heightened conceptual insights.

We believed we held the clearest vision of the perfect life provided by such significant mind altering chemicals like LSD, marijuana, and "special" mushrooms.

Discharge from the Navy occurred within a year. I stayed stoned, completely addicted to pot for the next 17 years of my life.

My addiction and new philosophies led me to rebel against all moral restraint. I indulged in a life of anything goes "free love," focusing my full attention on every fleshly desire set before me.

I erased my moral responsibility conscience by choosing to believe the argument presented by "new age philosophers" that God as creator and savior was dead.

I was further wanted to believe "enlightened" notion that God was a myth made up by ruling powers centuries ago to keep simple agrarian societies in their place; submissive and in control.

Their need for dominant control was the real reason for religion and the need for a "God of fear and imminent destruction" in its earliest origins. I had learned in my drug induced faulty reasoning to believe all the selfish, self-serving doubts about God and dismiss all my Christian educated beliefs.

Nine years into my first marriage, I faced divorce. Joyce did not agree with most of my new age beliefs. She rejected drugs because her stubborn nurturing practicality knew they were not legal, and imparitively, she could not function as a good mother to our daughters if she used them.

Her persistent conflicts with me demanding a cessation of my pot addiction and "lifestyle" met with stoned indifference. I made a few token attempts to comply with her wishes but failed to let go of my habits.

They were her demands, not my addicted behavior desires. The effects of many more layers of guilt, shame, self-doubt and cloudy pot dulled judgment brought me to overwhelming despair in the early fall of 1975. I planned and attempted suicide.

Even in my deepest moment of despair, I concluded that my daughters would be better off if they believed their Dad had died of natural causes in a fire. So heavily medicated with pot, I set fire to my home and prepared to end my life.

I see clearly now that even then, God still had a thread of claim to my life. After intentionally sucking in massive amounts of smoke, I lost consciousness. I woke up amid the flames with sober judgment and knew God gave me another chance to live.

As a consequence of that event, I faced a criminal charge of arson and was ordered to enter rehabilitation in a psychiatric hospital for severe chronic depression.

I recovered, dealt with my criminal charges, and received a probated sentence for my crime. Even in the face of all the evidence surrounding me that I was making poor choices I denied the cause and effect link of responsibility between my depression and my addictive behaviors. I continued to remain a captive of my drug and sexual addiction habits.

I divorced Joyce within two years. I walked out and left my family behind. In that decision, I had a new conflicted identity. I had not become the same angry man my father was.

I had become instead a man defeated and alone in addiction. I chose a simplistic solution and immediately dove into a relationship with another addict.

In all my years of addiction, I had one positive trait shaping my destiny. I had a strong positive work ethic. Even though I was a druggy, I continually held down good jobs in the computer industry.

I can only look back now with disbelief. I cannot imagine how I was able to perform at all in highly skilled analytical tasks. I continually managed to get by and satisfy the minimum requirements of my job demands.

However, I never excelled in the workplace where years of specialized training in the Navy could have left me primed for a successful life-long career.

Within three years of my divorce, I was again in a long term relationship. I was living with Marcia, my old sex, and drug pal. She left her first husband to be "rescued" by me. There is no doubt that we were beginning our relationship with all the worst motives.

We started immediately living a life of "adventure." Three years into our adventurous nomadic lifestyle, we were married.I declared to her "I do not know what I want to do when I grow up, but I want to have fun now."

At that distorted drug bound point in my life happiness meant rejecting my technical career. I decided instead to play and have a great time choosing jobs in the ski resorts of Colorado, beach resorts of Florida, and lastly, an adventurous life of a professional gold miner/prospector in California.

Six years passed, and I slid further and further into habits of isolation and rejection from anything and anybody that represented a stable norm.

My carefree lifestyle began coming to an end as the result of inattention to even the basic needs of my body, and I came face to face with the day of a sudden break in my altered reality.

Chapter 2

You Have Cancer! How do I cope with this death sentence?

When we begin our personal relationship, I am willing to meet you in your despair

"" In centuries past when humankind was less sophisticated, I established clear sets of rules for my chosen people to follow. I had them keep records of their progress in keeping to my rules.

Their history of following those rules is a sad story. I created humanity to be adaptive. Rules are needed guidelines in the making of wise choices.

I intended them to help you avoid making significant mistakes in navigating around continual calamities. I hoped all of you would learn the rules and appreciate me more because they did not have to learn as often from painful experience.

However, I also created in man's adaptive nature, the useful ability to learn the most valuable lessons from the greatest adversity.

Whatever adverse circumstance of living confronts the man defines his destiny. These conditions either end his existence, or they strengthen his knowledge and adaptability as he overcomes the adversity.

I created him to have the capacity to decide for himself how he will face adversity. He can rely only on his personal strength, skills, and knowledge if he chooses. He can depend on the collective strength and expertise of the community in which I planted him.

He can also decide to trust me and my love for him relying on my infinite source of strength and knowledge. The choice is his.

If he chooses path number 1 or number 2, he will face circumstances that leave him helpless to overcome the inevitable calamity.

His helplessness leads to frustration; frustration gives him cause to resent his situation, resentment leads him to become angry, anger leads him to strike out wildly at any source of adversity in a vain attempt to control the events.

In the end, His inability to control the outcome develops into a desire to shield himself from the possibility of another similar adverse event, and he spends the rest of his days fearing the next calamity.

His true protection is my responsibility. I have all of the resources necessary to do the best job. When any man tries to protect himself without me, He often fails miserably.

The emotion of failure produces fear. Sadly, fear further diminishes a relationship with me. Fear shuts down his ability to be a creative adaptive problem solver. He can only rely on limited past experiential knowledge.

His fear also blocks him from my ability to heal whatever wounds he receives from adversity and restore his peace and relationship with me.

If he chooses path number 3, I will be there for him. In the beginning, his relationship with me will be timid and uncertain. I will strengthen his thoughts and awareness of my presence with my creative wisdom.

I will surround him with others who are also choosing me to assist them. I will provide all the protection he needs so he can remain at peace. Finally, he will learn to trust Me as his provider and his friend.

One day, then many days, then for his long, productive life he will learn to honor me with his heart of love and genuine appreciation for My relationship with him and my for my provision."""

My gold mining occupation/ultimate escape led me to live in the Northern California mountain valleys along the Klamath River. There in a little town of 1300 souls called Happy Camp; I dredged the river for placer gold.

I was never vastly successful, but fortunate enough to be willing to spend six to seven hours a day six days a week underwater dredging up the river gravel to extract the small amounts of hidden gold. Every day, I would begin with the attitude that this would be the day of my "strike it rich" massive gold discovery.

I held firm to the notion that the next big multi-ton boulder I moved on the bedrock river floor would be the one covering my buried treasure.

I spent over two years dredging for and at least finding enough gold to make a small, simple living. Relentlessly self-reliant, I worked my body as if I were a man of steel.

During the last few months of my mining however, I began to experience pain in my right bicep. Even though it hurt, I forged ahead and continued my mining operations. Next, I started to notice a growing lump in the muscle. It was small at first, but as the weeks wore on, it grew larger and more painful.

Finally, the pain and the size of the lump grew to the point where I could no longer bare it much less ignore it. I went to the local doctor. His quick exam sent me 70 miles upriver to the nearest surgeon for a "closer look."

One week later, my return visit to the surgeon left me unprepared for the worst possible news.

"You have an extremely aggressive but rare form of cancer. I have scheduled an appointment with a surgeon in San Francisco. The best chance for your survival will be to amputate your arm at the shoulder".

I sat stunned and unbelieving of the gravity of his words. Then finally the gravity of his final words began to penetrate my shocked consciousness.

"If all of your treatments and therapy options work the best as possible, you have about a 50% chance that you will live for six months, maybe a year."

The impact of that moment and those words had only one other close reality stopping event to compare them to; it was the "who do you want to live with" question thirty-six years earlier.

Suddenly I was no longer an adventurous youngster having fun before I "grew up." I was a forty-year-old man who might not live to see His forty-first birthday.

I drove the seventy miles downriver to my tiny travel trailer home in silence. There was no way for me to peer through the shock of my pending reality. What would I do without an arm? What kind of life is this last year going to be for me? The questions kept coming, but the answers did not.

The next morning I knew my only chance to make sense of my new reality was to spend some quiet time alone. I chose to hike miles up into the mountains surrounding Happy Camp. I wanted isolation and some undisturbed quiet time to think carefully through what I was facing.

I picked a peaceful spot with a distant picturesque view and sat down to think. My preservation instincts told me that this was a moment requiring me to make a careful and considered assessment of my life.

I thought about others whose lives were ended abruptly without time for any evaluation. I began realizing that even though the future was tremendously uncertain, I was grateful for that moment of reflection and hope it represented for the possibility of a chance for a change in the outcome, or at least the beginning of acceptance of the end.

My first, assessment was to question my decision to live my vagabond life. Was my adventure decision worth my time and efforts? Was I honestly satisfied with my "playful, carefree lifestyle"? "Was this life valuable and fun"?

What meaning and purpose had it accomplished? I sat there in quiet thought. I could only carefully and tearfully conclude that all of it had produced little genuine satisfaction.

I still was not happy or satisfied with myself and the person I had become. I had spent all those illusive years chasing my dreams, and now my life would soon be over.

As I carefully considered my life for the first time, I began to come to terms with the truths of my future reality. I was going to die, and I had no idea what my life would be like for the next year and possibly more important eternally.

I also did not know what my eternal future would hold. The eternal future? Did I have an eternal future to consider? As I sat there, I had to go to the very heart of the spiritual life question I had chosen to ignore for almost 20 years.

What if there was a God? What if what I learned in my younger years was true? Certainly, I could not deny the fact that the world outside my reclusive existence continued to be a place of escalating hostility. I could not ignore the prophetic words in my bible classes of Christ's return.

How do I know for sure all the "enlightened" arguments about God being a just another myth were true or were those rational arguments the real myth I had come to accept without question.

They were plausible reasons but were those behavior excusing rationalizations honest facts. Was I willing to face the eternal reality of a life of torment in Hell just because I was too stubborn to admit maybe just maybe I was wrong? Wasn't I living a kind of hell in my present reality of being isolated from my family and my kids?

What do I know with absolute certainty? Am I so intelligent or arrogant to believe my own personal "knowledge" is greater than the wise minds of men for centuries before me?

Finally, I confronted my moment of humbling truth. I had to reject my conveniently held argument against God's existence.

The denial of His presence and awareness of my life had to stop. I had to admit I was excusing my self-destructive behaviors by denying the truth that I was responsible to God for them. I had to accept that He did in fact exist. I was forced to conclude I had been an idiot for not accepting Him.

The overwhelming evidence of His presence was all about me in the still peaceful harmony of the mountain forest as it stretched out before my eyes.

At that moment, I became a part of the peace of that majestic mountain scene. I was no longer an isolated man, a stranger, sitting in it. I was a part of its wholeness. Maybe I was just a dot by comparison, but still a part of it all.

God met there in the now humbled spirit of the honest humbled man left inside me. I walked down off that mountain that afternoon knowing I would be OK, whatever OK was. I knew I was no longer completely alone, no longer afraid to face the future.

That day was life changing. My understanding of God and His plan for my life was no more than a vaporous misty concept at best. Even as simple as my acceptance of Him was, He was willing to meet me at my most desperate point of need. He was there to bring me peace and simple assurance. His pure confidence that moment was good enough for me.

One week later I walked into the office of the San Francisco surgeon. I was prepared to accept whatever he had to tell me. I had said goodbye to my right arm. I accepted that I could figure out how to adapt to life without it. After all, other people lost their limbs in the war. They continued to live meaningful, productive lives.

I prepared for whatever the doctor had to say. He smiled at me and said he had the best possible news. My CT and MRI scans showed that the tumor had not spread anywhere else.

Furthermore, a third analysis and diagnosis of the biopsy tissue sample revealed that the cancer type grew from a much less aggressive cell origin. I needed to undergo radiation therapy after surgery.

Finally he finished the visit with: " I am not going to have to amputate your arm, just remove the tumor." I would lead a whole and normal life.

Now as I reflect back on that life changing event I might conclude that the misdiagnosis led me to a false sense of desperation the day on that mountain top. I could argue that the conclusions reached by the surgeon would have been the same no matter what I decided.

However, I knew the truth in my heart God had given me a reprieve. At the time I had no idea why He had given it to me, or what my second chance would mean, but I knew instantly that living my second chance life would be worth the effort.

Humbly and honestly experiencing the reality of those memorable days was the beginning, my first step, in a long journey home.

Chapter 3

My life is not working: Rejecting my life of Sex, drugs and rock and roll.

""As I begin to draw you to me through the patient power of My Spirit, You will begin to see your life for what it is.

My light will shine into your dark places, and you will find the courage to admit the destructive path your actions have led you down. I will be with you and give you the strength to walk away from that destruction.""

I would be lying if I said that everything was immediately better after my cancer treatment. I got a job working at the local lumber mill. I was making improvements in my stability, but I was still playing Russian roulette with my life.

I continued living a life of drug addiction, and a life of pursuing multiple sex partners. It was the addictive elusive chase for sexual fulfillment part of my life that finally brought me to a partial surrender.

That was the day I faced the reality of the end of my latest fling. The experience was at best unsatisfying for both my girlfriend of the moment and for me. In fact, it was much less than fulfilling.

Plainly, it was another total personal rejection disaster.

Marcia and I had an open sexual relationship agreement. We were not bound by normal agreement to live a life of sexual fidelity.

We believed another new age argument. Sexual freedom was the road to complete sexual satisfaction. The rest of the world, trapped in monogamy, was crippled by unfulfilling sexual exclusivity.

The argument sounded utopian. The books we read supported the idea of a new and healthier sexual/social norm. We were excited about being part of the vanguard. We were demonstrating and promoting a better and healthier uninhibited sexual paradigm for future generations.

I spent days trying to resolve my feelings of failure and self-loathing from my latest broken relationship. I replayed, again and again, the conclusion that none of my experiences had brought me any real happiness. Thoughts of suicide reemerged and held the dominant focus of my attention.

Finally one morning I decided I could no longer continue. Marcia and I awoke and started our morning ritual of rolling a joint and beginning the day stoned.

I sat there staring thoughtfully at the joint in my hand. Finally, after what seemed like hours, Marcia prompted me with the question of "Well, are you going to fire it up, or just sit there and stare at it all day?"

I had reached the final decision of failure about my addictive lifestyle. Either my addiction had to end, or my life had to end. I knew I could not have it both ways any longer.

I simply asked her if she wanted me alive, or if she wanted the pot. She chose me. We ceremoniously flushed all of our supply down the toilet and destroyed all the paraphernalia along with it.

Yes, the ideals of sexual freedom all sounded wonderful and alluring. Those utopian ideals, however, did not consider the messiness and unpredictability of human emotion in an intimate relationship. Casual sex is not casual, nor is it real fulfilling intimacy.

The truth I experienced was that every one of my sexual encounters was more than just the brief interlude. No matter how I tried, I could not separate my inner self and my appreciative emotions from the experience.

I naturally desired to bring openness and genuine pleasure into the moment. In each encounter no matter how transient, no matter how casual, I left a little bit changed by the memory of the moment.

I could not help but become emotionally bound by those real living persons willing to be that intimate with me. Those emotional bonds felt like a snippet of my life belonged to my partner of the moment and were then left behind not to be forgotten and sadly missing from the rest of my future life.

Part of me yearned to continue the relationship. Another part longed to experience more of the pleasure and excitement of new "intimacy."

I reflect back now, and my wiser heart understands my motivation. Part of me wanted the human acceptance I received from those moments. I confused a moment of risky trust as genuine validation.

I needed assurance of my worth as a lover to bolster my fragile and mostly fractured male identity and lifelong deep sense of insecurity. However, in those days of the wild pursuit of "happiness," I still wanted to be accepted and to be remembered as a worthwhile caring person.

The ultimate truth was that with every sexual partner, I became entangled in a relationship. Giving of and receiving intimate pleasure, no matter how "casual" the agreement of the moment, was not liberating. It was a confusing bondage of conflicting needs values and emotions.

Every encounter revealed the expectation of some coin of appreciation in return for the extension of intimate trust. . Sometimes it was a promise of future favor, or the unspoken expectation of provisional assistance, or the sharing of drugs.

Whatever the expectation, the cost of that entangled relational expectation was always more than the original casual agreement.

What my partner of the moment desired was to be honored and valued for our shared experience, but honor and value is learned over a long period of relationship founded on mutual acceptance and trust.

The hope of the immediate no strings attached payoff in true momentary intimate satisfaction was a myth. There could be no satisfying and lasting memory of the casual, intimate moment when the main ingredient; loving committed fully focused intimacy, was missing.

I have been free from the addiction to all forms of drugs for 29 years. I can truly say it was the best decision of my life. Did I make that decision with the help of intentional dependence on God? No, I made it using only my strength. I, at that point of my life, I was still my own God.

Yes, the mind can make and hold firm to a steadfast decision when there is sufficient motive and desire to change course. It can decide to change even if the change means giving up years of drug addicted behaviors.

Did I miss getting stoned for a period after the decision? The honest answer is No, I was relieved. I was glad that I could finally see the harsh reality of my life for what it truly was; a belief in a notion that was false, immature and untrue.

Do I regret all those years wasted chasing an illusion of a pot of gold at the end of an endless rainbow? Yes, however, I can easily live with those regrets more than I could live with my addiction.

Am I ashamed that I lived that life? No, there is no shame in admitting the truth and changing. There is only shame in remaining chained to addiction while denying its bondage.

Finally, did I make that decision to change by myself? In retrospect, I have to admit; I did not. I was not capable of giving God the Glory and appreciation for His influence at the time. I now must bear witness to His presence.

Without Him quietly patiently using His influence to give me the courage of self-examination; I would not have been able to either conclude that change was necessary or believe it was worthwhile.

God met me where I was. He quietly performed a master reset of my addictive habit pattern and set me on His pathway to peace.

Yes, Lord Jesus, You do deserve all the Glory. It was not self-reliance that led me out of addiction. It was you who so quietly lovingly carried me out. In that quietness, I didn't even notice your presence!

Chapter 4

Is this all there is to life? Here I am wandering in the wilderness searching for meaningful relationships and fulfilling love.

""Your new path will not be easy. You are still going to face challenges in your pursuit of the Love I have placed a longing in your heart to find.

I am the only source and satisfaction of the hunger for peace, unconditional acceptance and your yearning for the knowledge of your true identity.

You will search for and find none of these treasures until you are completely ready to surrender all of your life and Spirit to my care""

Within a few days of my decision to leave the drug life behind, Marcia and I returned to Texas and the sanctuary of my family.

In God's perfect timing, my younger sister Ellen and Her husband Dennis were returning to Dallas as well. Dennis had just retired from a 20-year career in the Navy.

Our mutual navy background and experiences helped form a strong bond of friendship between Dennis and me. For the first time in my adult life, I had a true nurturing caring man in my life as a real and trusted friend. Dennis and I had no personal agenda in maintaining our friendship; we just genuinely liked and valued each other.

Coming back home to my family was a wise decision, but the adjustment to relational living was still a struggle for me. The idea of getting a permanent job, and settling down to a normal life had little appeal.

I could not imagine in my defeatist mindset being accepted back in the technical world, nor could I imagine regaining the knowledge base to compete in the rapidly advancing technological age.

I chose a path of all kinds of self-employment. The first stable endeavor was a job as a janitorial subcontractor. Marcia and I could work nights and sleep days without the hindrance of children. Life as janitors worked for us and provided a stable if meager life. We had a home of our own and reliable transportation.

One of the vitally important parts of our life that did not change was an attitude of living in a committed monogamous marriage.

We still held on to the belief that open sexual relationship was acceptable behavior. However, the rising prevalence of sexually transmitted disease influenced our willingness to risk our future on casual sex.

The risk of life altering danger kept us from our past open pursuit of pleasure of the moment casual sex lifestyle. In another point of retrospect, we were both weary of the chase.

After nine years of marriage to Marcia, I was feeling a growing sense of resentment toward her. I was bound to her not out of great love, but out of a sense of duty. I could not imagine her capable of a life out on her own.

She was not the strong, motivated, self-reliant kind of a person who could survive well left to her resources. I felt irrevocably bound by her dependence on me to be her husband.

Several other strong attitude shaping factors were emerging at this same time in our lives. The first of those was Dennis's cancer. His doctor discovered a large tumor in his nasal passages.

Unfortunately for Dennis, there was no miss diagnosis. He fought the disease for seven years before losing his battle. Even through all the suffering he faced, Dennis remained my true and influential friend.

Our lifestyle and our attitude dramatically changed when we found much better employment in the trade show industry as commercial decorators. The work paid a craft wage, and greatly improved our standard of living.

After we had settled into our new occupation, a significant relationship shift occurred. Marcia's old college sweetheart and close friend Carl became a part of our household. Yes, I did say college sweetheart.

Marcia and Carl became lovers immediately after he moved in. The benefit for Marcia was that she then had the loving intimacy she desired. I had the benefit of better financial stability. We were then a household of three wage earners. Carl also joined the decorator's trade union and we lived and worked openly as a "threesome."

The evolving reality of our relationship, however, was Marcia's growing commitment to Carl. Her enhanced intimacy and attention to him meant a lessening affection with me.

I found myself feeling less and less a part of their lives. I could only sit and watch their growing love and committed intimacy, and know that I wanted what they shared for my life as well.

In reality, I could have achieved that kind of intimacy with Marcia. I had allowed my past biased resentment about her dependency on me to blind me. I could not appreciate her for the true and loyal friend she was.

The final chapter in my relationship with Marcia came shortly after Dennis's death. I had begun a new habit of spending time on the internet playing bridge. One of the side attractions of those games was the online chatting between players that developed.

I began chatting with a lady who lived in Canada. She also expressed her discontent in her marital relationship. The intensity of our online relationship quickly began to be the focus of my reason to play more bridge.

I didn't realize how much of a discontent and emotional isolation focused "dumb" decision I was making. I believed I could chase a dream of a relationship with this lady based upon the sensually charged content we were bringing to our online chatting.

I could not see that spending hours chatting on the computer does not foster a healthy relationship any more than having casual sex. Intimacy is far more about surrendered, commitment than about titillated personal feelings of the moment.

I spent several weeks with her in Canada before coming to the honest conclusion that my dream was no more than another shattered illusion.

The lasting result of the time in Canada was a change in my desires. The break in my connection with Marcia and Carl gave me the power to decide I wanted more to life than just sex.

I wanted to learn how to fulfill my deepening hunger for satisfying, loving relationship. I knew I craved genuine appreciative acceptance. What I did not know in my limited perception was the source of that unquenched longing.

I had no idea that God had placed that hunger within me to be satisfied only in intimate personal relationship with Him. In his perfect timing, He was steadily drawing me to Himself.

For the second time in my life, I made the decision to end my marriage. In retrospect, that decision was more about running away from commitment than running toward a promising future.

My lifelong habit pattern was" duck and cover," then run rather than do the hard work of self-discovery needed to change my underlying habit of protection from the pain of rejection I experienced as a child.

Chapter 5

Lord, draw me to you! I want to believe, but help me in my unbelief.

"" One by one you are led to untangle the ensnaring chains of bondage you have allowed for yourself. I have a plan for your Life, not to harm you but to bring you peace and a future. I have already chosen the right helpmate for you. She will be the next bright lamp for your path.

I know you have chosen to believe your doubts and doubt the beliefs I have written on your heart. Now is the time for you to break away from that choice and discover the path back to my heart. You will clearly see I am your bright beacon toward home.""

When I left Marcia, I knew I was running out of time in my life to make personal progress in finding enduring happiness for my future. Intuitively, I knew that my singleness was the best time for me to take stock of what character traits of my life pleased me.

I knew I wanted to strengthen those pleasing traits while eliminating the habits that produced the most conflict and frustration.

One of the base level areas I knew I wanted to improve in my life was the orderliness of my living environment.I decided I would rather have fewer material possessions in my life. I could be content with some carefully acquired decorations in my home as long as they had esthetically pleasing value. I had no desire to accumulate lots of stuff just to fill empty spaces.

I had plenty of memories from childhood during that defining time, of living in an environment of depressing clutter. I decided I did not want to repeat the frustration and discomfort in my future.

I knew I had not made the effort either as a child or an adult to correct the clutter. Instead, I lived with it until the level of mess was so overwhelming that cleaning it up required an army of help and a week of effort.

That simple desire to live a life of order has been one of the blessed desires that are an integral part of my present life. It amazes me how simple it is to maintain order as compared to the daunting task of restoring order.

I also knew that I did not want to try to find a new marriage partner from the "dating scene." The idea of spending hours hanging out in a bar or dance hall had no appeal.

I decided that I stood a much better chance of discovering an enduring life partner if I had the opportunity to know at least some basic nuances about their personal values rather than reliance on random chance "pick up" dating.

I chose instead to use an internet dating service. It was not perfect, but it did afford me at least basic elements of choice and control. After months of hit and miss trial and error encounters, I was ready to give up on the internet matchmaking idea.

I do not know with certainty what I expected, but I do know that I met a lot of wounded ladies with a lot of unresolved conflicts in their life. I am also sure they felt the same way about me.

At the same time, I was making the decision to give up this matchmaking plan, a lady on the match was quickly coming to the same conclusion. Her name was Laura.

She had logged on to discontinue the service when the computer matching option gave her my profile. She read it and decided to email me because she saw that I enjoyed snow skiing.

Laura saw that I lived about 70 miles away, and she banked on the distance to keep our relationship casual. Ah, she thought, a Ski buddy, who lives too far for any more than a casual relationship.

What she did not know was that I had recently moved less than 20 miles from her home, and forgot to update my profile information. Oops, my mistake. We began an email chat and got to know each other in discovery time.

We both enjoyed our email dialogue, so I gave her my phone number. Laura called me while I was working one evening, and we made a date for the next evening, Saturday, @ 5 pm. I was excited and drove to her home with a bouquet of flowers.

To my surprise, Her adult son Barry met me first in her driveway. He was washing her car. Barry greeted me warmly and extended a hand of welcome.

I knocked on Laura's front door, and her daughter Amy answered holding her ten-month-old son Ben. Again I received a warm welcome, and finally, I got the opportunity to present flowers to my date, Laura.

The first thing I noticed about Laura was her radiant smile. She set my flowers down, excused herself, and went to her bedroom and attended to the needs of Ben. I could clearly see her tender nurturing heart, and was immediately smitten.

I can only say everything about that evening was magical and amazing. From the moment I sat in the recliner in Laura's living room, and Hobbes the cat climbed in my lap and added his warm, affectionate welcome to the family my life changed. I knew what fostering a loving family ment to Laura, and I knew I was quickly becoming an accepted part of it.

Within the hour, we were sitting out on her front deck talking with Barry. He was telling Laura that he was going to have to see a doctor the next week because he knew he had a gall bladder problem.

When he told her the news, I took a moment and looked at Barry more closely. What I saw was something I chose to keep to myself. Barry had a distinct yellow jaundiced cast to his skin.

My past medical experience instinct convinced me immediately that he was more than just a "little bit" sick. My memories with Dennis were all too fresh to dismiss what I was seeing before me at that moment.

The rest of the evening with Laura was everything I could have hoped for in a perfect first date. We went to dinner, came back to her home, sat and talked for several hours on her deck about the real deeper side of our thoughts, beliefs, life perceptions, and emotions.

From the beginning, Laura was disarmingly transparent about her past life altering mistakes, and that allowed me to be just as open with her. We could agree that we were both flawed, and while those imperfections shaped us, but they did not define us.

What we could agree with most was that we did not have to live in the past and allow those flaws to shape our future. Those moments of quiet honest communication were the best place for us to start our relationship.

Laura also openly shared her faith with me that evening, and carefully expressed what an important part of her life Jesus was. I was thrilled at her profession of faith because I intuitively knew that having a relationship with her would be a path for me back to a life of faith for myself.

During the last 12 years of my life since my mountain top moment with God, I had allowed my marriage with Marcia to delay me in accepting a commitment to return to faith. Marcia was rebelliously agnostic in her spiritual knowledge. At best her spirituality was defined by new age spiritual sentimentality. She had no motivation to pursue any practice of faith that required commitment and action.

The last of the evening included a video and a long night of growing intimacy. I knew in my heart long before it was over, that I had found the woman I wanted to spend the rest of my days with, and from that first night, I made a lasting commitment to her.

One of the first boundaries that Laura established in our relationship was her commitment to attended church every Sunday. She made it clear if we wanted to have an ongoing long-term relationship; she was not going to attend church alone.

If I wanted a relationship with her, I was going to have to reestablish my personal life of faith. I readily agreed to her boundary, and the following week, we began attending her Church.

The first morning Laura and I walked into the Spirit filled pentacostal church wher she worshiped, I did not know what to expect about my experience.

The visit marked my first entrance into a sanctuary in 30 years. I knew my relationship with Laura was on the line. I also knew the principles of the Christian faith.

However, even though I knew all the facts about Jesus' birth death and resurrection, I did not know if I could truly believe and accept a life of religious belief and expectation again.

I had all of those layers of counter-cultural learning in my belief system. There they were in my mind reinforcing the basis of my skepticism about the "truth" of Christ. I was not even certain that His death burial and resurrection were a vital part of my belief.

Furthermore, I was ignorant of the idea of developing a personal relationship with Him, the Holy Spirit, and the Father. Moreover, I had no clue about the active presence of the Holy Spirit and what that could mean to my life.

Even with all my uncertainties, I was willing and eager to find God again. I knew intuitively finding my faith meant far more to me than securing a permanent place in Laura's life.

She introduced me to all her friends, including her ex-sister in law Carol, and Carol's husband Otis. I was surprised and in the same instant, pleased to see that she had not rejected the continuity of relationship with her ex-husbands family.

I will never forget my memory of the start of that service. I had been out of fellowship for so long. I was clueless about the intensity of Spirit-filled worship. When the first praise song began, I found myself looking around the room. My gaze fell on the face of worshiper after worshipper.

What I saw was both amazing and assuring to me. I saw true, sincere adoration as the congregation worshiped the God they loved. I saw their love being displayed openly and intensely without inhibition. I saw an attitude of honest and reckless abandonment in praising their Creator. Their faces lit up in joyous expression of adoration.

In that instant, I knew I would have no problem finding God with that same intensity for myself. I was flooded with a sense of relief and with a new emerging excitement within my spirit.

Jesus had come to meet me in His House of Worship and Praise. It was not an empty house of endless rules and restrictions. It was a House of Joy. Yes, I could see He still had standards of inner behavior, and I had a lot to learn.

I would have to take years of correction to my old habits to embrace those values fully. But I was sure God would lead me there one step at a time through the power of His Spirit.

I knew I had returned home to him, and embraced Him, the loving living God, for the first time in my life. What Laura's uncompromising boundary for her life and relationship did for me was set the stage for our personal relationship to grow. She also set the stage for me to grow in my person maturing as well.

I would be leading you into a fairy tale if I said that we lived happily ever after from that moment. The truth of all committed relationships is that even in the most perfectly compatible couples, there are still biases of experience. They set the stage for differences, disputes and boundary issues to raise their conflict in marriage.

The reality of past experience bias was no different for Laura and I. We were coming into our relationship from two entirely different poles of habit, background, and thought.

Laura's life focused on her family and her faith. She was a carefully structured perfectionist in all of her personal and home life habits. She had carefully decided from an early age to follow a feminine meticulous and perfectionist life. Within the bounds of her life and home, there was no room for new ideas or carelessly chosen habits.

A relationship with her meant adopting compatible habits or face the consequence of an unhappy wife. There was no room for anything less. Laura perceived any compromise of her standard as evidence of my lack of love and commitment to our ongoing relationship.

From my side of the street, I had spent 53 years not having to take a firm and disciplined control of my personal or relational habits, and I had no knowledge of how to begin changing them.

I could be found at any given moment chasing any bright and shiny object that would distract me from the path of my intentional task at hand, and Laura always instinctively knew where to look to find me in my wanderings.

I do not know the number of times Laura has had to pray; "Lord I know I asked you to bring me a Godly husband, but does he have to be such a raw specimen?"

I knew that I had a life of submission ahead of me to learn over time how to change my habit nature. I also hoped that over time, some of the most pragmatic characteristics of Laura's nature would begin to soften because of my more pliable laid back nature.

Our relationship has conflicts and adjustments. I admit that again and again, my poor skills in responding to those conflicts has been a source of periods of discouragement and lengthy periods of depression.

The slovenly and embarrassing unpolished flaws in my character did not have me well prepared for a smooth adjustment. I had so many personal biases to rid myself of, and no skill or insight about where to begin the process.

I did have however from the beginning of our relationship, the unshakeable perception that God had placed me in Laura's life for His reasons. I knew I was in the place He planted me.

I will also admit; I had no idea what our life together would look like, or what levels of personal commitment I would be required to make in maintaining our relationship. The beginning of our first major adjustment challenge came swiftly, but not from an entirely unexpected direction.

Chapter 6

Your Son, Barry, has cancer! The loss of a son, and a shift of paradigm.

"" The burden I have for you to carry is light. I have prepared it for you so my power will do all of the heavy liftings.

However, if you insist on carrying it yourself as you journey on the rocky path relying on your strength, you will find little rest.

I have prepared this part of your journey to help you see I never intended for you to replace me as provider, protector or comforter to these precious souls I have bound you to in love.

One day you will see. Clearly, I am your refuge and your strength.""

The memory of the minutes we spent sitting in the surgery waiting room while Barry was in surgery is an indelible part of my relationship with Laura. We had only been together for two weeks when her only son announced that the surgeon he had seen decided that Barry had a compromised gall bladder due to a clogged bile duct.

Another surgeon was called in to perform a complex surgery to salvage Barry's gall bladder. The surgery was to take about 6 hours.

There were about a dozen of us family members who gathered to await the results. In less than an hour, the nurse came to us and said the surgeon was available to consult with us.

We were all surprised and went into the conference room. The compassionate look on the surgeon's face was pained, and serious. The Doctor simply said that when he had a view of Barry's abdomen, He saw all the signs he needed to stop the procedure.

The mass that had been detected the day before was cancerous. The source of it was Barry's pancreas. He went on to say that there were many small tumors in the abdomen that indicated that the cancer was already spreading to other organs.

Barry's prognosis was bleak. There was no known cure for pancreatic cancer, and patients usually succumbed within a few months. Barry was 29 years old.

The truth that tugged on my awareness two weeks earlier was confirmed. I knew for sure from that moment on that God had placed me in Laura's life. I was there because I had experienced firsthand the loss of someone dear to me, and that loss was still painfully fresh in my emotional memory.

I expected that I could be the solid, heroic, rock of a man that Laura needed. I could provide comforting and protection for her. I had no idea how unprepared I was for either that large an assignment or how much my expectation of being there for her was self-motivated by my need for her acceptance of me.

I had no education or understanding about the process of grieving. I also had no idea that there would be another quantum level of emotional pain that Laura would be facing in losing her child.

Often I would try my best to comfort her over the next year Barry lived. She would look at me with contempt and tell me I had no idea of how much she was hurting.

She was right I did not, but I did what I could to be there for her and all of our family. I could not change the reality that Barry was dying, and Laura was grieving deeper than I had ever experienced grief.

From the beginning of the unfolding drama of Barry's battle with cancer, I decided to do all that I could to reduce as much additional stress on Laura as I could. I was only a little more successful at living up to that huge task.

There were endless days of serious concerns that needed to be tended to as we made ourselves available for Barry's deteriorating condition. We delayed personal plans and focused solely on Barry's needs of the day.

The only plan we did not delay was a commitment to each other in marriage. We married in our home December 24, 1999.

Our marriage was accepted completely by all of the family. Even David, Laura's first husband was a part of our life along with his second wife, Laura. I found myself warmly received into a close-knit family that was now even closer as we all did whatever was needed to be available for Barry.

Laura and I continued our commitment to serving the Lord by regular church attendance throughout the year, and we agreed to attend premarital counseling.

We talked about our goals and the commitment we were to make to God in the joining of our lives. I was completely agreeable to attend the counseling. I knew I was not skilled in being the husband I wanted to become.

One of the piercing questions asked of me by our counselor was about how I was dealing with my past marriages, and how I felt about them. I said I was ashamed that I had tried and failed, and that I would do my best to make our marriage work.

There I was still speaking out of and stuck in a self-reliant point of view. I believed the strength of my personal unaided efforts could make all the difference it would take for our marriage to succeed.

Our counselor asked Laura, "Does Bill understand the concept of God's grace?" Laura said she wasn't sure I did. I sat there listening to the question and her response, but the implication of my awareness of how important that understanding of grace was flew right over my head.

Instead, I thought; Grace, hum, I don't know what they are talking about, but it probably isn't so important that I need to take the time right now to study and understand it. Oh, how short sighted and closed minded I had allowed myself to become all for the purpose of "being there" for Laura. I was willing to put my learning and spiritual maturing on the hold without examining the consequences of my "get it done" mentality.

We continued to focus our attention on the immediate needs of our life and Barry's condition. Tending to those left no time for good solid communication or the opportunity to talk through growing conflicts and disagreements.

The decision to bury all of my personal needs and desires became a constant low- level source of discontent and bitterness within me. I deferred to Laura's expressed desires in the major and most minor decisions of our relationship.

I believed I did so because I wanted to bring her happiness and more stability in the midst of our shared crisis. While I was annoyed at having to change my life so dramatically, I argued with myself that it would be worth it in the long run.

I also argued with self that I had decided during my singleness about desiring to in the pleasing environment that our home together was becoming.

I would rather have the annoyance of unsteeled conflict than live the unsatisfying and frustrating life of clutter that I had experienced for all my previous years. I decided I appreciated the difference.

The result of all my efforts met with many successes, contrasted with bleak failures. There never seemed to be an end of the demands on my time or the extent of the expectations required of me as I deferred to Laura's choices and plans for my time and financial commitment.

To sum it up, I was not ready for the task that God had laid out before me. I worked at it, but many times with the obvious wrong motive and therefore not a whole heart of commitment the task required.

No matter how hard I tried to compensate for the growing gap between Laura's expectation and my inadequate personal performance. I could not satisfy her desires.

Dissatisfaction in our relationship was not an insurmountable problem during the first six months of our marriage. There were always plenty of Barry's need to distract me from focusing on my feelings; however, it did influence in me a general sense to conclude "I was not good enough" to meet Laura's needs.

Thirteen months after I began my relationship with Laura, Barry passed away. Laura's burden of grief grew, and it was not something I was prepared to deal with to the level she needed.

She was in the anger stage of grieving, and I did not even know she would have those intense emotions. I also did not have the insight or skill to cope or help her cope. I allowed her anger directed toward me to become internalized. I owned those emotional moments as clear signs of my personal failure.

I concluded that surely I was doing something wrong, and my inept ability to meet her needs was the true source of her dissatisfaction. I did my best to cope, but on my strength, I was not doing well.

Laura and I started attending a marriage encounter group at our church to help us get through the rough spots of those first 12 months. However, with Barry's passing, we discontinued attendance.

It only took nine more months of the anger and grief dynamic to take its grip on my commitment to my marriage. I felt like the progress of resolving our conflicts had stopped, and the building malcontent had shown me that once again I was not capable of sustaining even my third marriage.

I Packed up and left Laura, once again running away from commitment. I could justify my need to run away more than I could deal with the pain of the rejection I felt.

The heart of the problem was a rejection of myself, and my identity as a "looser." Those self-worth issues were the unspoken basis in my decision.

I spent two weeks separated from her, and once again spent quiet time reevaluating my life. The one prominent truth I began to discover was that I held the highest appreciation for the genuine person Laura was.

I remembered the good and tender moments of our relationship. Those memories were the best I had ever experienced in married life. Sure the poor moments hit record lows of disappointment and pain, but the pleasure and love we shared were more genuine than I had ever known.

I knew I would be a fool not to make my best effort to work on our relationship. I returned home and asked Laura for forgiveness for leaving.

Laura's acceptance of my return was conditional. She wisely observed that we needed all the help we could get in rebuilding the love and trust in each other.

She asked if I would agree to follow all the way through the intimacy training program, and also if I would agree to attend a weekend retreat called Tres Dias.

I also knew I had more than exhausted all of my personal resources to find working solutions to our marital dynamic, and I was more than willing to have whatever fresh insight and counsel that was available.

I did not know what I agreed to in full, but I wanted to give our life my best shot. I signed on to both programs, and only had a week to wait before attending a men's Tres Dias weekend. I had no comprehension of what God could do in my life in the course of three short days.

Chapter 7

No sacrifice is too great. It is my turn to salvage the life of another child and her family from drug addiction at all cost.

"" Your experiences are unique to you. You will encounter others I have placed or planted in your journey who have similar experiences.

I placed them there so you may minister to their needs with a heart of compassion. Learn to discern the open and willing heart.

I have drawn the humbled hearts to me. You are to be my hands, my feet; my love made real to them. Love them in their brokenness bind their wounds, and allow me to provide for their strengthening through your leading.

Guard your heart so that you do not fall prey to their weakness. Look to me for your perfect words of encouragement. Remember still; I am the source of their provision through you. Use the abundance I give to you wisely.""

During the first six months of my relationship with Laura, I had little contact with Laura's youngest daughter Wendy. She lived with her husband and two young children about 90 miles North West of Dallas in Wichita Falls.

The brief amount of time Laura and I had visited them in their home was sadly disconcerting. Their environment was chaos clutter and poverty beyond anything I had experienced.

Wendy told us Darren had lost his job, and there was little income available for them to survive on. She had no idea of how they were going to put their life back together. What she did not say was why he had lost his job. We learned later it was because he had been arrested for possession of methamphetamines with the intent to distribute them.

On the way back home Laura expressed her overwhelming disbelief at what we had witnessed. Her maternal drive to fix the problem took over.

We talked about what possible improvements we could make in their home environment to give them a needed boost of encouragement. She concluded that the cause of the wretched mess was because Wendy was obviously just depressed.

Several weeks later just before our marriage, the truth came out about Darren's drug problem, His arrest, conviction, and sentence of ten-year probation. All the details had been kept secret from the family.

Wendy and Darren's tearful and contrite admission of their problem found fertile ground in my heart. I recalled how many years of my life I abused drugs.

I reasoned that if I had been able to break out of my addiction; with a little help and support, so could Wendy and Darren. I had no firsthand knowledge or experience of the power of "meth" addiction.

I also had no knowledge of the strength of physical dependence it produced. Once again my heroic habit of blind compassion and the absence of any rational plan on their behalf swung into high gear.

That night I made a commitment to Wendy as her future stepfather to do whatever we could to see them through their crisis.

It was not long before that commitment had them moving into our new home. There we all were filled with the hope of beginning our marriage. We viewed it as the fulcrum of the healing that needed to take place for our children and grandchildren.

What had begun was the start of the most difficult and exhausting paradigm of my life with Laura. We both wanted the best for Wendy and Darren, and equally, as important, we felt a compelling need to provide a stable environment for our two adorable grandchildren; Five-year-old Sheyenne, and 18-month-old Tate.

We both felt we had no other choice than to take them in. We further justified our decision by believing it was the loving Christian thing to do.

We would be the positive influence in their lives that would be the best nurturing environment for them to make a new start. We hoped by providing it Darren would find the courage to continue living a drug-free life.

To boost my income and support a larger household, I changed jobs and started a new career selling roofing jobs for a residential roofing company. That job change decision quickly morphed to starting a roofing company of my own and provided work for Wendy and Darren.

I believed I could be a strong influence in their recovery, and in the process show Laura that she had picked a real hero for a husband. I started the business with no working capital and just enough money to buy tools and supplies for the first job.

We managed with much frustration to complete some jobs, but I was not prepared to deal with the roofing client problems and train a raw crew as well. The venture failed in less than three months.

Wendy and Darren had little money left to show for their time working with me, and they continued to live with us as I did all I could to provide for the 6 of us for the next six months.

The main anchor that helped us maintain our commitment was the strengthening of our faith through our experience with the Tres Dias movement. We made a major level of commitment of our time in already busy lives.

Laura and I eagerly joined the group of workers who planned and labored at the task of producing the Tres Dias weekend events.

Among the most positive personal benefits for me was the fellowship of a group of Christian Men who accepted me with open arms and true Christian brotherhood.

For the first time, my commitments to those brothers and sisters in the community of believers met with appreciation and generous encouragement.

I knew that I was someone doing something important for Christ and that my contributions to the Tres Dias movement were making a difference in other people's lives.

The core purpose of the organization is to raise up strong spiritual leaders for both the Christian community at large, and for the Local churches. The plan for that leadership development is carried out in two phases. The introductory phase of first-time attendees and the longer term training phase of working as part of the team who plan and produce each three-day weekend event.

For each weekend we attended and worked, our experience was both life and heart changing in the overwhelming growth of our personal faith and personal relationship with God.

In the period of our first five years of marriage, we accommodated The Darren, Wendy and grandkids three separate times. It took us some time to become aware that the addiction problem was not just Darren's, but also Wendy's. There were several incidents where Darren had his probation revoked because of a failed drug test.

Our unwavering acceptance of them and their addiction without shame or blame place us as the first and on most occasions the only place of refuge in their crisis of the moment. After all, isn't that what Christian service to your family is all about?

During their second stay of almost a year, Laura found a double wide mobile home for sale at a reasonable price. We purchased it for them, and I made the land inherited from my father's estate available to them to place it on.

From the beginning of their life in their new home, there were still signs of weakness in their home life. The overall care and cleanliness of their new home soon paralleled that of what we saw when I first met them three years earlier.

Laura and I worked continually trying to find the balance point between being an encouraging support and enabling them in their addiction. The reality was that we far too often erred on the side of enabling them.

The most pervasive excuse for our choices to continue their support was the undeniable interest in maintaining a stable environment for our grandchildren.

What we did not recognize was how skillful their parents had become in weaving the needs of their children into the central focus of their pleas for assistance.

We were in denial of how much they had come to rely on our empathy to get by. We responded without requiring any real progress in the changing of their addiction habits.

Three years after they moved into their home, Darren faced his second offense of violating his probation. He came to us and said he had begun attending AA, and that he sincerely wanted to straighten out his life. He said that the environment in and around his home was so drug infested that he could no longer remain there.

For the third time, we opened our home to Him and the kids. Wendy did not want to move. She said she wanted to separate from Darren, and possibly seek a divorce. The whole mess of their lives was Darren's fault. He was the cause of their difficulty.

We rented a larger home to accommodate them, and I hired Darren to work with me in my two-year-old handyman business. I do not know how we made it all work, but day after day for two years, we strived to keep the bills paid, and have a decent home environment for them.

We believed that we were doing the best possible thing for the family. We spent time daily, counseling and encouraging Darren. He continually deflected responsibility for his circumstances.

He argued that whatever was going wrong in the situation of the moment was always someone else's fault. The ongoing dialogue was so pervasive that often we would resort to tag-team efforts at trying to help him.

The ultimate reality is that we could not help Darren solve his problems because He did not want to solve them himself, and he never felt desperate enough to press into careful self-examination and acceptance of his responsibility.

He stopped going to AA soon after moving in saying that he could handle his recovery. Outwardly he was showing signs of recovery, but he did not have the desire to commit to real change. He did, however; to the best of our knowledge remain drug-free.

Wendy, on the other hand, slid further and further into a habit of isolation and separation from her children and us. She would spend long periods of absence, punctuated with a series of late evening visits whenever she needed something that she could get us to provide.

It is easy to see in hindsight how manipulated we allowed ourselves to be. Laura responded out of her mother's nurturing heart, and I was expected to agree readily to help with the need of the moment.

The long-term result was to see our financial stability grow increasingly weaker. No matter how hard I worked, there was always more need than resources.

Chapter 8

Despair to rage. Take my life, the only way out

"" Do not hide the broken places of your life to from me or those who I place in your life for growth and learning. Your enemy will use them as weapons of condemnation against you.

Look to me for the protection you need when you are willing to admit your faults humbly so that you might heal.

Do not rely on the passage of time to cover your mistakes. Time will only delay the truth and plant the seed of mistrust into the heart of those you deceive.

Remember in your most bitter conflicts; I am your refuge and your strong tower of protection for your heart. I am here to heal all of your broken places. Learn to trust me for you are my beloved child""

The toll the growing awareness of our financial weakness grew apparent and mushroomed into a real crisis when my work van broke down. The van was beyond repair. This incident happened right in the middle of a handyman project.

I pressed Laura's car into service to finish the job amid many protests and misgivings from Laura. Don't mess up my car was her earnest concern.

Naturally, because of my haste to finish during the first day of use, I made an error in judgment. I hurried to get back to the job after buying some lumber; I jammed a board into the front windshield and cracked it as I closed the rear hatch.

I sat on the hatch opening frozen with dread. What kind of reception would this development get from Laura? My dumb fear born decision was to avoid telling her. Two days later she noticed the crack.

I made a bad situation worse and denied any knowledge of it. Wrong, wrong, wrong, decision. I allowed my fear of her anger with me to hide the initial truth and then compounded the problem be denying any knowledge of what had happened.

The result of my fear and stupidity was to spiral downward into guilt, anger bitterness and a massive sense of rejection. The episode was capped off by being berated as a liar by Laura over the phone as she drove our grandsons to school.

My mind focused on the rejection, and disproval she was teaching those two boys about me. My personal value and self-respect vanished in a moment. The conversation ended bitterly.

I allowed my anger to turn into unchecked rage. I slammed my cell phone onto the garage floor and saw it shatter into a great scattering of small pieces. Shocked at the result of my rage, I stood there staring at what promised to be another round of condemnation from Laura for my burst of anger and loss of self-control.

I felt undone as an avalanche of guilt, shame and condemnation washed over me. I could not see any hope of recovering from the intensity of my actions. I remembered vowing as a child to never allow myself to get to the level of rage I had just manifest. I had seen the tragic results of it far too often in my Dad's massive tantrums.

There before me lay the body of evidence of another pending marriage failure. I felt in that intense moment that my third marriage was over. I searched within myself and found no hope for anything in the future I could cling too.

Laura and I had spent three years working in the Tres Dias movement. They were some of my brightest moments, but not even those bright moments could balance out what I had just done. I decided I had nothing worth living for, and began contemplating taking my life.

My convictions arose about my eternal future, and I went on my face in despair before God asking for His help. That prayer went from asking for His help to asking for forgiveness for what I felt compelled to do.

I took all my prescription anti-anxiety meds and everything else I could find in the medicine cabinet and laid in bed waiting for the end.

Instead of "the end" I heard Laura's voice asking why I was in bed in the middle of the day. My incomprehensible answer led her to the immediate conclusion of "Bill, What have you done?" What have you taken?

Her anger and contempt at the scene of her pathetic husband rose with every word she spoke. Her final command was for me to help her get me into the car, or she would call an ambulance.

I could only follow her demand thinking quietly to myself that I couldn't even follow through with this decision successfully. The evidence of my own self-loathing lay on me like a mantle of shame and regret.

Once again, God's divine intervention came to my aid. He was much more able to provide for me in this new moment of brokenness than simply providing forgiveness. He used the opportunity instead to show me the tenderness of His mercy and loving kindness.

The first experience of His mercy happened within a day. I had been attending a men's Bible study and discipleship group with a hand full of my Tres Dias brothers for three years. We met every Thursday morning at 6 am.

The next morning was Thursday, and the dear brother of the group who took me home with him after my emergency room visit left me no option. I was going with him to attend the morning group fellowship.

The thought of facing criticism, disappointment, and condemnation of the sin of suicide loomed large on my thoughts. However, I resigned myself to face whatever would come along.

After all once again, there I was Shadrack, Meshach, and Abednego, being thrown into the fiery furnace of self-condemnation. The group's words of judgment could not be worse than my own.

To my amazement, there were no words of condemnation or judgment. Instead, these Godly men surrounded me, laid on hands in love and asked God for his divine intervention in breaking the stronghold of the spirit of depression and the spirit of suicide.

Furthermore, they asked for His healing of the self-condemnation I was struggling with and for the burden of it to be lifted from me.

They devoted the entire hour to this single purpose. I walked out of that home with every burden lifted walking in God's peace instead of the enemy's condemnation.

I awoke early the next morning and lay quietly in bed. The Holy Spirit had not finished ministering to me. My entire awareness became focused on a vision of the time of Christ. I saw Jesus, the Son of man, ministering to a man and healing him.

The truth the Holy Spirit revealed to me in that scene was that Christ ministered healing to the heart of the man first, and restored it to His peace. Then He asked the man if He wanted to be well.

The simple question focused the man's mind into the agreement. Finally, in the authority of the father, he commanded the man's body to follow through with their agreement.

I lay there amazed at the crystal clarity of what I was experiencing. One moment later, my attention focused on a scene of His disciples going out in twos performing their healing ministry. Once again, I clearly understood the revelation of the principles of the healing process.

In the next instant, I saw myself, and some of my fellow Tres Dias believers in Christ doing the same thing and achieving the same results. For the third time, I was in awe. Wow, we can still do that today!

Finally, the Spirit revealed to me the condition of my own heart. He revealed how I had readily believed the lies of the enemy about my future, and about the condition of my soul and my relationships.

He revealed that my heart was bound and burdened and constantly under siege. I felt the burden of readiness and vigilance to the possibility of the coming disasters and an insecure future.

I saw clearly my decisions of expecting rejection, isolation, unworthiness, and doom. In that intensely healing moment, He showed me He cared about the weight of all those conclusions of doom and rejection. I broke into sobs of relief as he cleansed them from me.

I lay there in brokenness from what I had just experienced and simply surrendered to Him. I prayed Holy Spirit I am not capable of clearly taking on the task of deciding what my future thoughts are going to be.

I want you to help me decide to reject all the limiting junk I am so prone to accepting without more than a few moments of passing thought.

From that moment on, He was true and faithful to be that lamp. Never again have we ever allowed my life to slide back into debilitating depression.

The far more life changing result of those moments was the emerging realization of God's unlimited power to heal the submitted and hopefull trusting person.

In the midst of my greatest season of despair, The Lord was there carrying me once again. This time, however, He had my full attention.

What God provided for me was example after example of acceptance and compassion. I continued to grow in my abilities as a leader in the Tres Dias movement. I followed through with each assignment with a new courageous zeal and passion for God's power to restore me.

The closer I walk with God, the more I learn that He does not give life awareness lessons without follow up. He always provides me with time to practice the new lesson soon after learning it.

Within a few days after my visionary morning, I received a call from a dear brother. This compassionate man asked me to be in prayer for his wife, Candy.

He told me she had experienced a mild heart attack the day before. Her Doctor had scheduled her to have heart surgery the following week. I agreed to pray and asked Laura to be praying as well.

The following morning I awoke with the overwhelming burden on my heart. I knew I was to encourage and lead a special prayer session for Candy. I also knew the best time for prayer session was just before the closing ceremonies of the upcoming Men's Tres Dias weekend.

I related my burden to Laura; Her brow wrinkled, and she said. "Bill, you don't even know Candy." However; I could not shake the press of the Spirit to follow through.

God was also working on Candy's heart as well. She did not believe in spiritual healing. She was a strong, self-reliant business professional. Candy believed that God provided trained doctors for healing.

In her personal prayer time, He birthed a desire for her to trust Him for the best outcome. The Lord assured her there was a moment of His perfect timing coming for her complete healing.

She accepted His assurance with quiet expectancy.Through Gods providence, we met the following morning at church. Laura and I had just walked through the entrance doors when we heard a familiar greeting used within the Tres Dias community of believers.

I had never met the person who was greeting us however; I knew this smiling lady standing before us was Candy.

I told her of the burden I felt to have a special intercessory prayer time for her later in that day. Her eyes brightened, and she readily agreed. That evening as we met, one of the first priorities was to call for that prayer time and lay on hands for Candy's healing.

God in his loving kindness held us to a small group, Candy's best friend, Laura and myself. Simply and earnestly we prayed for God's healing for Candy's heart condition.

She kept her appointment the next day for surgery. Her amazed doctor could only conclude there had been a misdiagnosis as he reviewed the results of a healthy heart EKG.

I see Candy occasionally, at Tres Dias events. She flashes me a knowing smile. We both quietly give God all the glory he deserves!

Chapter 9

What goes up must come down. Broken ladder broke back.

""I greatest desire from you is more than your belief in me. I am not a myth or legend, I am!

Your life is most secure when you learn to believe me and my word. You can trust me in your most desperate moments. I will never leave you nor forsake you"""

A year and a half passed after my season of despair. Laura and I were still working on maintaining our day to day focus as caregivers for Darren and our grandkids.

The stabilizing of my emotional and mental well-being helped a great deal to foster my willingness to take on the task of providing a home for them. I had no idea how long their need for provision would last. I did not have any idea that they would be with us for almost two years.

One of the ongoing challenges I faced was scheduling and providing enough work to keep both Darren and myself busy. When there was not enough work, I would do the work myself, no matter what the task.

This decision to handle even the toughest tasks by myself when necessary brought me to my next point of crisis in a little more than a year.

It was nearing the end of summer on a hot Texas afternoon. I had one task remaining to complete a long list of tasks for a homeowner. My task was to climb onto the roof and paint the large brick chimney with the same masonry paint we had painted on the rest of her brick home. Because it was the last day on this job, I was alone.

Without a single care, worry or thought, I set my ladder up on her driveway, grabbed the 5-gallon bucket of paint and proceeded up the ladder. I knew I could complete the task before the end of the day.

I was glad to be finishing and was mentally preparing for my next job. Suddenly all of my plans and thoughts of the moment vanished as I reached the final step before stepping onto the roof.

To my panic, I heard a snap, and then suddenly felt the support of ladder rungs disappear from under my feet. In a flash, I dropped the paint bucket and reached for the gutter in front of me. I could only brush my hands against it to straighten my plummeting body.

One moment later, I felt my heels hit the pavement 14 feet below. Immediately I sensed a loud snapping sound that echoed through both my brain and my body. I felt white hot searing pain through my back as I collapsed into a large puddle of paint on the driveway.

As I lay there gasping for air, I knew I had broken my back. I struggled in my paint soaked surroundings to lay myself flat on the ground. All I could think to do was begin yelling for help from the homeowner.

I yelled and yelled with no result. Finally, I realized as I lay on the hot pavement that I was going to have to find the strength to roll over and crawl to her door for help. I do not know how I made those thirty feet, but I did, and thankfully, she answered.

It seemed like forever for the ambulance to arrive. I was overwhelmed with both the pain of my back and the emotion filled reality of what I had just happened. I knew a broken back would be a life altering event.

Memory after memory flooded me of friends who had hurt their back. They would let me know quickly that because of the injury they were not to perform any heavy lifting or manual labor. How could I expect my outcome to be any different?

The paramedics who attended me had a light-hearted sense of humor as they stared down at my pathetic paint-covered body. Their cheerful disposition and smiles helped to lighten my mood.

We joked on the way to the hospital about meeting a fire unit with a big hose to wash me down before getting to Baylor emergency room.

There in the midst of the uncertainty, God provided me with much needed moments of the humorous relief I needed to break the stronghold of fear about my future.

My brave lighthearted front held up for a little while until I locked eyes with Laura. She had just walked into the trauma center where I lay waiting for treatment. When I saw her, I began weeping bitterly, and repeating, "Honey I'm sorry, I'm sorry, I'm so sorry!"

Laura looked at me with confused bewilderment, and simply asked: "what are you sorry about"?

"Laura, my back is broken, I sobbed, and I know I am not going to be able to be the provider our family so desperately needs" I broke into a rush of tears and grief.

"Bill, what makes you think God who has brought us through all the tough times we have had together is going to drop us now just because you can't work? "

Laura's question pierced me to the core. I stopped dead still and thought. I could not in any way deny the compelling truth of how often God had carried us through tough seasons.

"You are right, sweetheart. Let's lift our burdens to the Lord right now" We began praying earnestly for His assistance and His comforting assurance. We asked Him to replace all of my fear and doubt with His love and peace.

As believers, we often say God is an "on time God." Right then and there God was on time. The next moment I received a phone call from my Tres Dias brothers who were anticipating my help that evening.

One of my leadership responsibilities for the Tres Dias community was to supervise the facility set up for an upcoming Men's weekend. I explained my plight to this brother, and a room full of my godly men went to their knees on my behalf.

God's power to answer prayer is amazing. The emergency room had been a scene of resounding chaos and yelling. Across the hall, there was an out of control patient who was screaming in rebellion. He was resisting all attempts to calm him.

Within a moment, the entire emergency room area was peaceful, calm and still. The contrast of that stillness to the chaos was God's first answer to my need.

His peaceful assurance declared His first victory. I knew I was in His hands, and all was going to be ok however it turned out.

Within a few minutes, the attending trauma doctor walked into the room. "Mr. Billard, we are going to admit you. You have a compression fracture of your first lumbar vertebra. That is the vertebra just below your rib cage.

We are going to wheel you out in the hall before sending you up to surgery. We need this trauma room for another patient. I will be out there in a moment to talk with you about your treatment."

I have always had a sense of awareness that my body always tells me what I need to know about its condition. I knew from the first moment of pain my injury was severe. There was no doubt in my mind about the extent of my injury.

So now, what was going to happen because of it? Those were my thoughts as I lay in the hall. There was one thing I was now trusting with certainty.

I knew about God's uncompromising capacity to provide for all my needs. I knew my need of the moment included quick and complete restoration of my back.

I shook my head in amazement as I realized what a few moments of prayer, the encouraging support of Laura and my brothers provided for me once again.

"Mr. Billard, I need to discuss your treatment options with you." My doctor resumed her conversation where she left off earlier. "You have two options; you can agree to surgery. I have called a neurosurgeon who is scheduling you for surgery this evening if that is your choice. The surgical procedure will be to fuse the crushed vertebra to the one above it.

"There is another possible option is for you. If you are strong and healthy enough, you can wear a full back support body brace. You will have to wear this brace for about 6 to 9 months. There will be confinement to bed rest and rehab most of that time. I recommend the surgery for your condition. The choice is yours."

"No, I have three options" I spoke carefully and confidently as I began to proclaim my personal choice boldly.

The surprise on her face was clear. "Oh?"

"Yes, my third option is for God to heal me perfectly and completely. That is the one I am choosing."

Her expression broke a little into a bemused but patronizing smile. "I understand Mr. Billard. You must understand that we can deliver two options of treatment. You must decide between them.

The surgery staff will be down in a while and talk to you. Meanwhile, I have given orders for the nurse to give you a shot of morphine to ease your pain. There is one more thing you must do right now. You need to lay perfectly flat on your back. The smallest movement could be fatal."

"The fall crushed the entire top of a vertebra, and one wrong move could damage or sever your spinal cord. Do you understand?" Oh, what sobering thought of reality! I soon drifted into a partially aware state from the effects of the morphine.

It seemed like forever, as my sense time slowed before anyone came to attend to me. I lay quietly waiting for admission and the surgery staff visit.

Finally, a young man came and told me he was taking me to my room. I asked him when the surgery staff would be talking to me. He said they were involved with another surgery, so I was going to my room first. I waited all night, and no one from surgery appeared.

Early in the morning, my floor nurse came into my room. Mr. Billard, it is time for your morphine shot. I looked at her and made a clear and firm decision.

"No, I do not want to take any more morphine. I want to be alert and fully aware instead. It is what I need so I can be an actively praying for my healing from God."

My nurse smiled and said she understood, however when the pain got too much for me to bear, she would come and give me my morphine.

Immediately, I began in earnest to lift my needs to the Lord. I knew I could stand on His promises to never leave me or forsake me. I also knew that His word said that "By his stripes (his suffering) we are healed." I believed His word and trusted Him to restore me.

The mid morning hours passed, and still, there was no surgery interview. After a short time, the intensity of my pain climbed. With each passing minute, however, I continued to lift my needs to the Lord. Quickly the top of the list of my needs was for relief from the relentless pain.

The door opened once more, and I heard a familiar soft and tender man's voice. There with me was one of my best friends John. We were close friends in the Tres Dias ministry.

John was a Chaplin for the Baylor Hospital system. He said that He was assigned to Baylor central for the day, even though he normally worked the suburban hospitals.

I knew in my heart his change of assignment was no coincidence. God who tenderly loved me and cared about me had provided John to be there.

He knew the special bond we shared would minister strength and encouragement that morning. Together, we thanked and praised Him for His faithfulness.

More of the morning passed, and still no surgery team. Instead, there was a stream of special people who God had given a divine appointment to be present with me. They were brief moments of respite and shift of the focus of my attention to the now level 10 pain I was experiencing.

Still, I held fast to my commitment to be fully awake and aware. "Lord, I am weary. Please let me just close my eyes for a few moments and get some rest."

It seemed like only a few moments passed when I opened my eyes again, but those must have been a few minutes of deep sleep because I was not aware of anyone else entering my room.

When I reopened my eyes, there before me on my bed stand was the answer to my prayers for healing. My attention riveted on a small red blanket folded neatly and tied with a red ribbon.

I did not have to wonder about the purpose of this blanket. I knew exactly where it had come from, and why it was on my table. My memory flooded with the hours Laura, and I spent with our brothers and sisters in Christ.

We had continually over many months during worship services lifted the blankets up to God praying for the power of the Holy Spirit to inhabit the stack of gift blankets.

In those prayers, we were standing on God's word described in the book of Acts when the early church prayed over handkerchiefs and aprons and distributed them to the sick.

Our congregation witnessed the power of Holy Spirit presence in the anointed blanket to heal the afflicted. I knew that healing had been a bedrock testimony of the blanket ministry of my church.

I also knew the pastor had to drive over 100 miles round trip to bring it to me. He saw me asleep, and quietly completed his mission of divine appointment.

Tears of joy washed over me as I covered myself with the precious gift. I praised and thanked God for His perfect ministry to me. I knew in my heart at that moment that there was a divine reason why I had not seen anyone from surgery in the sixteen hours since my admission.

I felt completely secure and protected under that simple blanket. A brief time passed, and I began having an incredible urge to roll over on my side.

I sensed that I would be more able to endure the pain if I did. So I rolled on my side, and suddenly, I was aware that all the pain vanished. Not just some relief, but complete relief.

Once again tears of joy flooded over me followed by many more prayers of praise and thanksgiving for God's deliverance.

Moments later, my door opened again. This time, my visitor was the emergency room doctor who had admitted me.

Her voice was sharp and alarmed as she said "Mr. Billard, what are you doing on your side. Don't you remember I told you to lay perfectly flat on your back!?"

I looked up at her and smiled, "Yes I remembered what you said, but do you remember I told you that I had a third option? God is fulfilling His promise, and His healing has begun. My pain is completely gone; He has taken it all away."

I looked into the face of this dedicated young physician. All she could do was gaze intently back at me.

Finally, she said, "Excuse me; I am going to make a phone call. I will be back in a few minutes."

When she returned, it was with a completely different attitude and demeanor. She met my eyes with a smile. "Mr. Billard, I have just conferred with the neurosurgeon. We think there is a possibility you might be a good candidate for a body brace instead of surgery."

She explained in detail the pros and cons of both treatments. She told me that it would be at least 6 or more months before I could return to work, or longer if it required strenuous physical labor. Finally, she concluded, "The decision is yours."

My response was "Well this is not going to be a hard decision, fit me for the brace."

An amazed nursing and occupational therapy staff tended me the next day as they placed the body armor like brace around me. I was required to get up and walk around the ward, and as a final test, climb a flight of stairs.

I accomplished every requirement with complete ease and comfort. I had been pain-free for over 24 hours. They agreed I was ready and immediately sent me home.

The next day, I began returning to my normal routine of life. I spent all day participating in a Tres Dias ministry meeting.

The lay leader of that meeting, a physician, could only shake his head in amazement at my progress. Four days after a major injury and God had me up and functioning normally.

Two days later, I returned to my work as a handyman and spent the next ten days remodeling a master bathroom. I never missed a day of work.

After only one visit to the Doctor, I discontinued wearing the brace in the second month of recovery. I felt so confident about my healing; I never returned for any further follow-up.

My family never had to suffer from lack of provision. Because of that trial, I learned the most valuable lesson of my spiritual life. I was not my famlys provider nor was I ever intended by God to believe that provision was my responsibility.

It is not mine, nor is it the validation of my male identity. In the months ahead I learned God was and has always been my provider. I am merely a conduit He uses for His provision to flow through. His provision is enough for me to share with all the lives of all those He places in my care.

I emerged from that healing experience fully aware of God's divine intervention in my life. More so, I emerged a stronger and more confident leader in ministry, and in my life.

Even more important, I emerged confident that I served an awesome God who loved me unequivocally, and that I never had to worry about His presence or intimate interest in me and the circumstances of my life.

My story could end here, and God glorified in the truth of this testimony; the truth about His personal loving interest in each of us moment to moment; the truth of His divine wisdom.

He created our bodies to respond and adapt to the direction of the desire of our heart especially when we agree with His plan for us.

However, GOD in His wisdom knows that I am a "slow learner of spiritual truths. I have been aware since my college life that learning anything can happen one of two ways, I can either learn by repetitious exposure to the new information, or I can learn from as little as one or two very intense experiences.

Emotionally intense experience sets the stage for the most indelible learning. Such an event was just over the horizon from the experience of my broken back.

Chapter 10

Are you all right, do I need to call an ambulance?

""Consider it all joy when trials come. They are the testing of your faith.

I have prepared you for them, and they will assure you of my presence and love for you, for I know the perfect plans I have for you"""

My next lesson in God's awesome power came a year and one week after my back breaking lesson. It was once again a sweltering hot day in August.

I had been working on a job performing extensive repairs to a large home. I was close to completing my lengthy list. Completion of this next task required coordination with a roofing replacement work crew at the home.

The job appeared to be proceeding normally. I was in the process of making repairs to an old open wood frame arbor covering a large deck. In the space of a few moments, the task went horribly awry, and the arbor structure attached to the back of the roof started to collapse.

Are you OK, Do I need to call an ambulance?

I had no idea why I was being asked such an important question with such an urgent tone of alarm and concern. I opened my eyes and became aware that I was laying on my back staring directly at the sky above.

It took another moment me to remember the past few moments. Why was I laying on the ground? I thought I must have slipped and fallen as I made a last ditch attempt to protect the house from major damage of the collapsing arbor.

I noticed a massive support beam lying close beside me.
My attention shifted to assess why I might need an ambulance. I felt no pain, nor could I sense any reason to be concerned.

"I guess I had better get up and show this guy I am OK" I said to myself. I tried to stand, but nothing happened. I was still lying on the ground. I tried to move again and was bewildered as nothing happened. I tried again, and again, still nothing.

Finally, I came to terms with a new reality; none of the muscles from my neck down were going to respond. I realized that this voice was right I did need an ambulance because there I lay, completely paralyzed.

And so began another chapter in my journey in experiencing the healing power of God's love.

God in His wise plan for my life had prepared me for this moment. The memory of my despair from my last accident had been written indelibly in my heart. More important, the memory of the truth that God was right there with me was even stronger.

I simply closed my eyes and prayed, "Lord Jesus, I desperately need you to be everything for me at this moment. You are my comforter, you are the provider for my family, you give me the wisdom to know what to do right now. I lay every burden at your feet."

The words of that simple desperate plea etched themselves in my heart.

The next moment the Lord gave me His unmistakable reply. "I know the plans I have for you, plans for your welfare and not calamity to give you a future and hope." The promise of Jeremiah 29:11 also etched itself in my heart clearly unmistakably linked to my prayer.

Immediately I was bathed in a sense to peace and calm expectation. As before when I cried out in desperation, I knew I was going to be all right.

The Lord turned my thoughts to his plans for me and my agreement to be the lay leader of an upcoming Tres Dias weekend in the spring.

I simply ended my brief prayer with Him by declaring; "OK Lord, if you still have those plans for me, then I know you are going to heal me again perfectly and completely."

I opened my eyes and looked at the man whose voice of concern had brought me to the startling awareness of my condition. "Yes, you do need to call an ambulance. I am paralyzed and cannot move at all."

My voice was calm assured and completely at peace as I directed this wide-eyed man to take care of all of my immediate needs including retrieving my cell phone and calling Laura so I could tell her what had happened.

I directed every need in a quiet, detached and calm voice of a care provider, not the panicky calamity struck victim of a life-changing event.

I spoke out of an unshakeable confidence, certain of my destiny as preplanned for and shared with me by God Himself.

Instead of fear and dread, I was focused, aware, and quietly anticipating what God was doing and what He had just assured me He was going to do.

The first evidence of His assurance was the paramedic who attended me. He was upbeat and positive and kept giving me encouraging thoughts of the temporary nature of my paralysis.

He did this despite the overwhelming physical evidence and a without any prompting from me. I lost no time agreeing with this careing man and Giving God the glory for what I knew He would do.

When we were on our way to the Hospital, He said that our destination was Baylor Hospital downtown. In my heart, I groaned. I thought how ironic it was to be going back there again a year later with another major injury.

To my surprise, the ambulance came to a stop on the freeway. The driver said that we would have to divert our destination and go to Parkland Hospital because the traffic was at a standstill ahead. Silently, I thanked the Lord for His tender mercy.

If I had been an average resident of the Dallas area, the news would probably have met with a disappointment similar to the one I had experienced minutes before. However, I welcomed the news with a heart filled with joy. Parkland hospital was not a strange place of fear and dread; it was a place familiar to me.

God was bringing me to a place I trusted. I knew it was a place of refuge, safety, medical excellence and compassion. In my heart, I felt as if I was returning to the security, and source of my first experience with healing and fundamental understanding of medical practice.

We wheeled through the ambulance entrance. I knew how I would be received and evaluated by the staff. I was alert, focused, and able to answer all the attending doctors questions clearly and fearlessly.

I described the circumstances of being hit with the support pillar and made it clear that I had sustained another accidental injury to my spine the year earlier.

I also shared with them my humble appreciation of coming home to Parkland emergency. That appreciation brought knowing smiles of agreement from my attendees.

Their care and evaluation were thorough and swift. Test after physical test of my limbs and torso met with the same evaluation; this patient is unresponsive to stimulus and is experiencing a complete loss of reflex and motor control.

As they were conducting their evaluation, however, a new sensation began gripping the focus of my attention. It started when a nurse was taking my blood pressure. The placement of the cuff on my arm, felt as though someone was stabbing me with a knife.

The pain was unbearably intense, and I asked what was happening. The doctor told me the nerves of my arm were attempting to send stimulus signals past the damaged nerves causing my paralysis.

In a short time, that same kind of intense pain began to mirror all over my body as the insulation effects of sudden body shock was receding from my awareness.

My doctor told me I would have to endure the pain for a little while until the clinical evaluation was over. I closed my eyes and asked God for His strength and endurance.

Laura arrived just a few minutes later and came in to be with me. She was a welcome sight and relief all on her own. I thought of the similar scene a year earlier and smiled at the memory.

My smile assured her that God had us covered. She told me that she had put out a prayer request on the internet to the Tres Dias communities and that she had called some of our close friends and Jim our pastor.

The ER doctor admitted me to the ICU. He told me that I had an injury to my spinal cord. The injury was the result of a whiplash condition that occurred when the heavy support beam struck my head and forced it backward.

He went on to explain that I had an arthritic condition of my spinal cord column that made it narrower than normal, and that condition made the damage more severe. Finally, he said that he would give me some morphine for pain.

While I still lay in the ER, a stream of encouragers and prayer worriers began to arrive. The first was Jim. He looked at me and asked me if I believed that God could perform another miracle in my life.

I told him that I was praying for it and counting on it. I shared the word I had received in my first prayer for healing an hour earlier. He began to pray in earnest for me and anointed me with oil as He prayed in the spirit.

One of the touching memories of those first few hours was when Laura told me that our dear friends, Marvin and Mary dropped what they were doing, and drove 90 miles to come to the hospital to be with Laura and I. They arrived less than an hour after I arrived in the ER.

The Bible teaches, "The fervent prayers of the righteous (compassionate loving and caring) accomplish much."

I remember being transferred to ICU, and into my bed. I looked up to see the nurses attending me surrounding my bed. They looked like angels with their hair silhouetted and glistening in the indirect lighting.

I sensed again God had carefully planned another confirmation moment. I settled quietly into my new surroundings.

I know that ICU is a place where the patient has limited visitors and is supposed to be restful. However, my night in ICU was neither limited to a few visitors, nor restful.

All evening long, I had a parade of my friends in Christ visiting with me. They encouraged me and lifted me up to God for healing and comfort.

I remember hearing the patient in the bed next to me. He continually cried out, "Senora, Senora, help me." Those mournful cries echoed in my ears throughout the night. I spent hours praying for this man who was in such hopeless despair.

The most memorable and affirming events happened hourly. My nurse would come in and put me through a series of muscular response exams.

By midnight, I began to experience the return of some of my right-hand feeling and function. It felt good to begin to grip in response to the nurses prompting.

Her smiles and assurances were even more encouraging and helped me to focus my attention on the task at hand. I began to strive for more and more movement. I spent unceasing time in prayers of intercession and thanksgiving for every sign of my returning muscle control.

By morning my right side was strengthening, and I was able to begin moving my right foot and leg. After the morning shift changes, my new nurse came in to give me another shot of morphine.

I looked at her and said I wanted to try enduring the pain without help. I told her about my back healing experience, she brightened and left me to my prayers.

A short time later my unknown friend in the next bed had a female visitor. I was glad to hear her comforting tone as she visited.

After a short while, I heard the deep male voice of his doctor who began speaking to the lady. He asked if she could speak English, and if she would translate his assessment to the patient. "Tell him that he broke his back in several places and that he will never walk again."

Tears streamed down my face as I once again began lifting him up in prayer. That was such a powerful moment for me. Through the night I witnessed my condition steadily improving while next to me laid a man who was in such despair.

That man had to accept the assessment of his doctor as the permanent condition of his life. I knew in my heart next to me lay a man with no hope. I still remember him in moments of silent intercession. In those prayerful moments, I humbly praise God for my wholeness.

It did not take long for the rising pain level to gain the focus of my attention. When my attending doctor came to assess me, I asked her if there was any medication that would target the nerve pain, and still leave me fully alert and aware. She said that there was something that she could order that would help.

She said she was very encouraged by the progress I was making, and that if being alert and aware would help she was all for that plan.

God is amazing. He is attentive to the smallest details of our lives. After my doctor had ordered my new pain med, the nurse came back in and told me that it would be a while before it was available from the pharmacy.

She also told me that the special sand bed that the doctor ordered for me when I arrived was available. I was improving so rapidly that the doctor decided to cancel the order.

Every assessment, every visit, every prayer in those first 24 hours was part of His divine plan of provision for me. By evening, I had begun to have some response in my left leg.

My nerve pain med had finally arrived late in the evening, and I was feeling a little more comfortable. My pain level was still higher than I had hoped for, but I accepted that God had a reason for me to endure it.

The nurse came in and told me intensive care treatment was no longer necessary because of my progress, and I would go to a spinal injury ward for the rest of my stay. By 10 pm I was in the quiet of my room on that floor.

Laura told me she too weary from being up all night herself, and she was going home to sleep. I assured her that I would be fine and that I too was going to sleep.

My new ward nurse had just finished her muscle response exam. I had made no more discernible progress since leaving ICU. I still had little muscle control in most of my left side and no responses from my left arm and hand.

Laura told me my grip in my left hand was weaker than a baby. She kissed me goodnight as I began to drift into sleep.

I heard my door open before I could fully drift off, and a soft female voice inquired; "Mr. Billard, I am sorry to disturb you, I know you are in a great deal of pain, but I am from the lab, and I need to draw some blood. Will that be ok with you?"

I nodded and kept my eyes closed as she began her task. Once again, I was almost asleep when I felt the tourniquet release and a much more courageous voice declare; "Thank you, Jesus, Thank you, Jesus."

I came fully alert, looked at her and smiled."I can tell you love Jesus as much as I do."

"Oh yes, she said, but will you please forgive me. I am usually full of encouragement and ministering to all my patients. Tonight I am weary. I am a single mom with three small children at home, and I only got about 4 hours sleep before I came to work. Then I had to work a double shift, and this is my fifteenth hour on the job."

My heart melted with compassion for her as I remembered my experience with double shifts in the ER. I looked up and said. "Can I lift you up to the Lord for him to strengthen you for the rest of your shift?"

Her eyes brightened, and she said; "Would you do that for me? I know you are in a terrible amount of pain."

"It will bless me mightily to do pray for you." I took her hand and began to intercede for this Godly courageous young mom. The Holy Spirit descended upon me as I prayed. I knew it was Him praying through me. My dear sister in Christ thanked me and left me in prayer.

There are no other moments in my life where I have ever felt closer and more connected to the presence of God. I first saw myself lying on the ground the day before. My thoughts focused on the moment when I closed my eyes and surrendered my burdens to His care.

As I relived the moment, I became aware the Spirit was revealing to me I was seeing was life or death defining the moment.

I knew instantly in my heart that if I had not given Him complete control, I would have been at best like my helpless ICU roommate. At worst, I would have concluded in those first few moments of awareness that I had sustained a fatal life-ending blow.

My overwhelming shock and fear would have spiraled to despair and death, a victim of intense shock. Tears began streaming down my face as I began proclaiming my thanks to Jesus, my Lord, my Savior, and my healer.

The next moment, The Spirit began giving me clear sight about what I needed to pray to complete my healing. I understood that my entire body had sustained a complete surprise blow. I had been wearing a wide-brimmed straw hat and never saw the falling beam.

The Spirit showed me that I should start with the fingers in my left hand. I needed to assure them they could go back to the original form, function and plan God created for them. They could release the fear that held them captive because God's word says, "His perfect Love casts out fear."

As I began praying this simple prayer and focusing my attention, my fingers immediately began responding and moving.

A thrill of courage ran through me as I continued. I prayed for my hand, then my forearm, and then for my upper arm all with the same enthralling results. As my upper arm responded, I immediately raised it toward heaven and began praising God again and again.

I continued praying for every other affected part of my body still underperforming with the same outcome. Finally, I prayed the same simple prayer to my still painful spinal cord and nervous system. The next moment, all the pain had left me, and I sat straight up in bed.

The Holy Spirit made it clear to me that my belief in the simple truth that Father God had designed my body to heal in response to the intensity of my thoughts was vitally necessary for my bodies response. It had no choice but to submit to my intentional and fervent prayers.

I believed in His complete and perfect power to reset those damaged nerve cells and restore me to full function.
I lay back down, and the Spirit showed me friend after friend, and their specific needs and I lifted them up in intercession.

Once again sweet tears of joy, wholeness, and intimacy with my Creator and Lord covered my face as I could now focus my attention on the needs of others rather than my own.
I drifted off to a few moments of fitful rest.

Again the door to my room opened, and I looked up to see my floor nurse enter the room. With the joy of a kid in a candy store, I asked her to come around the bed to my left side.

She did, and I asked her to stretch out her hand toward my hand. I lifted up my hand and gave hers a power filled squeeze.

Her eyes widened, and she said, "Oh, my gosh!"

The ear to ear grin on my face was worth every ounce of her surprise. I shared with her those treasured moments of healing and then sat up got out of bed and walked around the room with full control of my body.

I asked her if she was a believer, and she said she was, and we both began proclaiming God's glory.

My final treasured moment of that night was when I went out to the nurse's station and spent time witnessing to the nursing staff about what a great and awesome God we serve. Finally, I walked back to my room and fell sound asleep for the rest of the night.

Two days later, I walked out of Parkland Hospital. I knew, without any doubt, the hand of God had once again restored me.

I have shared with you now the most awe producing moment of my life. I will never be able to express how much it has changed me until I am before the throne in Heaven.

I wish I could tell you that from that moment on, my walk with Christ was one of perfect oneness. I cannot, because, like any other person, life presses on.

My need to pick up the burden of family and home responsibilities as was pressing as ever. After a few weeks rest, I went back to my normal life of a handy man. However, one basic part of me had changed. I would be forever confident that whatever task or plan or purpose God had for me, I was ready to take it on.

I had that confidence because I knew that He would be right beside me every step of the way.

If there could be any lingering doubt in my mind about the truth of God's loving healing, two facts about those healings wash it away.

After my admission to ICU, The attending doctor had a conference with Laura. He mentioned his awareness of my crushed vertebrate. He had ruled out any connection between my present condition and that old injury.

More importantly, He admitted that if he had not known of the injury, he would have missed seeing the evidence of it on the scans. The crushed vertebra reformed and there was only a fine hairline scar on the bone where the new bone had grown to replace the crushed portion.

He stated he had never seen that before because the common re-growth process from compression fracture was pitted and jagged. He told laura that wild growth was the primary source of the chronic pain experienced after vertebrate injuries.

Laura could only smile and declare that "God doesn't do sloppy work."

The second confirmation came from my personal research born out of my curiosity about what I had just experienced.
I researched "central cord syndrome" injuries on the internet and found a lot of information about my kind of injury.

Patients who are young have the best outcomes. Most of those patients, after about 100 days of intense treatment, can learn to walk and to feed and dress themselves.

When a patient is over 50 years old, the percentage of recovery reduces to less than 1 in 5 even though the average treatment period is over a month longer.

I found no information or accounts of anyone walking out of the hospital after only three days and resuming a normal life.

The truth of the matter is that God blessed me with healing beyond anything that I could have ever imagined. I know that God placed me in exactly the right circumstances to bring me to the awareness, knowledge, faith, and trust in Him I needed to recover as completely as I did.

You may ask, did He do this for me because I am special or singled out to be an example to others? The answer in my heart is yes; I am special to Him because I am His child. God grafted me into His family because of the sacrifice of Jesus, not because of anything I have done in my presonal strength.

However, I am no more special than any other of His children. He loves us all and is willing and ready to heal each of us from whatever afflicts us.

Chapter 11

God's plan for my life, a search for meaning out of chaos.

""You are beginning to realize I am the fine crafter of your perfect life plan.

I bring you a clear vision of submitting to me as a servant, leading others out of my agenda and anointing. And the first shall be last, and the weak shall lead the strong.

Follow my leading and I will break your chains and bind you firmly to me. I will bring you healing to the oldest of your broken places.""

How do I use this once broken body to serve the one who restored it so perfectly?

There is no way for me to state how profound an effect my healings have had on me. For the past nine years, I have had a burning desire to share my experiences with others.

That desire does not come out of an attitude of conceit or pride. It comes out of a heart of humble gratitude for our magnificent Creator.

My desire to share this with you is solely for the truth of giving God all the credit and glory. What I have experienced is unusual in the eyes of the world.

It is especially true in our culture of "medical magic" go to the doctor and its fixed the with a pill. However, I cannot help but observe that we are quickly and surely facing a different reality.

In the coming reality, there is a clear line of distinction between the haves' and the have not's in the demand for and delivery of medical care.

The cost of care is above $10,000 per year for a family of four. With approximately half of American families producing their income from self-employment sources, the number of corporate covered insured families is dwindling as the median family income drops to levels lower than the mid-1990's.

There is no capacity for those families to provide the practical and hopeful answer of medical treatment. So what is the alternative? If you are one of the uninsured, what do you do next? Do you simply lose all hope that you are going to survive whatever disease or calamity awaits you or your family members?

If so, you will spend the rest of your days living in fear waiting for that disease or calamity. My hopes and prayers for you are to arm with new insight. Be inspired by what you have read, and use it to transform your choices.

Investigate as carefully as you can. Peer into God's word and discover his promises for you and your family. Come to know with unshakable confidence; you have a clear and powerful alternative.

You can ask the greatest physician of all for His second opinion about the treatment and outcome of your condition. You can believe in His unconditional, never changing, the perfect moment to moment intimate love for you.

Receive the healing he has planned for your life since the beginning of time. We in our human condition may not be able to wrap our minds around this kind of planning. Just believe the Lord does all the planning necessary. We do not have to understand it all. We just need to see the first step and leave the rest to Him.

All we need is the glimpse of His power to heal as it relates to our personal experience. We just need to be like Hansel and Gretel, being vigilant for the next breadcrumb of evidence He leaves in the pathway. Those precious little clues of His presence lead to full discovery to Him and the Pathway Home.

You may be wondering about those plans that God had for me. The plan that sprang to mind in my moment of surrender was the plan for me to be the lay leader of a Tres Dias weekend. I fulfilled the commitment, and the serving blessed me beyond measure.

What I could not see at that moment was that He had an even larger plan for me in the Tres Dias ministry. Less than a month after my healing, I was asked to lead the organizing of a new Tres Dias chapter on the east side of the Dallas/Fort Worth area.

With a population of over 6 million people, we knew we wanted to reach and serve more members of the body of Christ. Within a year, we organized and held our first set of Tres Dias retreat weekends in the service area. I had the humbling honor of leading that new community as its president for four years.

Now God in His wisdom has me on a new adventure of personal growth. He has helped me see that I have wounds and scars from my early years that leave me with places where spiritual and emotional healing are still needed.

He has an answer for those wounds as well. I am now focusing my spiritual attention to the recovery of those wounded places in my life through the Celebrate Recovery ministry movement.

The healing that I am discovering is profound. I was not even aware that I had need of the kind of healing I am receiving. In simple terms, I denied that those painful experiences had a limiting effect on my capacity to be the transparent, compassionate, and the Spirit led man of God that He planned for me to be.

The greatest and most growing part of my Celebrate recovery experience has been participating in and completing the 12 steps of the recovery process. These are the same twelve steps that are a part of all 12 step recovery programs. However, CR recognizes that all of us have broken places in our life experiences that put dents and bruises in the Godly character God is working to perfect in us.

I was able to embrace the process of recovery to help me win a victory over the most profound flaw in my character. I suffered immensely from a compelling desire to be accepted by others no matter what the personal cost or sacrifice to myself.

I had traced the beginnings of this flaw in my character to those early days of childhood when I strived to please my Dad to receive my validation of worthiness from him. My desire for validation devolved into a perception of rejection.

All these years I have struggled with this central conflict. "Who am I"? Am I worthy of being accepted by others? In not having the answer to those two central questions, I adopted a cope as best I can strategy.

Both at the conscious decision level and the unconscious emotional level I chose to adopt an attitude of striving to be the best I can be in my primary relationships no matter what the personal cost. I made those choices without seeking guidance from God in prayer.

I believed following this strategy would keep me from facing the possibility of being rejected. That basic strategy of compensating for my deepest feelings of insecurity was my largest stumbling block preventing me from being the best spirit led leader in my home and personal relationships.

Over and over in my life experience, I worked diligently to control the outcome of my relational experiences by striving to be an irreplaceable asset to the relationship dynamic. In the result, no matter how hard I strived, the rejection, whether momentary or permanent, would inevitably occur.

I would once again be devastated by the pain of it. I would in spite of the overwhelming evidence of the failure of that strategy continue to forge ahead with the same plan until all of my resources, physical, mental, material and spiritual, were used up.

Only then would I admit defeat. Even in those moments of crushing defeat and resulting depression I still believed my failure was as a result of my not trying hard enough or worse not being worthy of the love I wanted so desperately to share.

When Laura and I were married, I continued to use this same strategy in our relationship. I adopted the attitude that this is what God required of me to be a "Good Christian."

After all isn't turning the other cheek and not engaging in conflict what Jesus taught us? Aren't we supposed to martyr ourselves for Him? Doesn't the Christian world honor those who sacrifice themselves for the sake of harmony and peace?

I added these valid-sounding arguments to my arsenal of convictions of why I was on the right path in this all out effort to please others life strategy. Sadly enough, even with these entrenched arguments in place, I fared little better in dealing with the central conflicts and challenges that presented themselves in my married life.

One of those biggest conflicts was the continuing and never ending demands of making up the ever present deficit in the need for the provision of our daughter Wendy's family.

I believed that the lifestyle adopted by Wendy placed her and her children at great risk, and the possibility of death or long-term injury to them was a real and ever present danger that I needed to fix in whatever way possible.

I believed the possibility of any of the negative outcomes I imagined would overwhelm Laura, and ultimately end our life together.

I do not know if any of these thoughts I have shared sound familiar with your personal life as a reader, but there was enough evidence in the lives of others around me to convince me those possibilities were very real, if not inevitable.

In a perfect world, I would have been able to provide all the resources necessary to place the necessary hedge of protection around my family members. However the world we all live in recent years is anything but perfect.

This reality left me completely unprepared to face those additional burdens. My income continued to shrink from my business, and at the same time, the demands for more help escalated.

With the weight of those burdens, I felt more and more inept and incapable of being the husband and father I was supposed to be. The frustration of ineptness turned to the root of resentment toward the source of the extra demands.

Late in the fall of 2010 just before Thanksgiving, Laura announced that we were going to accommodate Wendy and her family into our household one more time. Wendy and her husband Darren contemplated divorce.

I had no idea at the outset of my agreement to their move in would be the new dynamic of our family life. The reality of it was that the grandkids moved in along with three dogs, two cats, and three guinea pigs.

While Wendy moved some of her personal possessions into our home, she adopted a habit of spending every night with her boyfriend in his place of residence. Therefore we traded roles and became the adoptive parents to our twelve and sixteen-year-old grandkids.

The other unanticipated dynamic was the continual demand for our family car as the source of transportation for Wendy. Over the period of 6 months, Wendy's use of the family car went from first a request, then to a privilege, it escalated further to a right as a family member, and finally an "expectation of the first right of need entitlement."

During this transition in her entitlement attitude, I paid little attention to the accommodation the demand required as we always had my work van as alternative transportation.

During the same period, our household provision continued to dwindle as the economic fallout of mass recession deepened. I pushed further and harder to find more job-related resources as a one week after another our situation grew tense.

The inevitable eruption of our family dynamic finally occurred. The long repressed resentment I carried; the additional unending burden transitioned from resentment to frustration to anger and finally to bitterness at my loss of control of my family, personal and relational life.

The entitlement use of our family car was the trigger that led me to two separate incidents of bitter conflict and anger with Wendy. The second incident escalated into a moment of violent assault upon me by Wendy and her boyfriend.

That incident was witnessed by her daughter, and placed me in the saddest outcome I have experienced in my adult life.

I could have reported the assault incident, and pressed a charge against Wendy. I could not do that, and further damage her life and the lives of her kids. Incarceration is not the solution for every poor choice of action. I was not going to be the one who initiated such a bleak outcome.

The exact opposite outcome was in store for me instead. Sheyenne, who witnessed the intensity of our conflict accused me of soliciting her to expose herself to me when she was ten years old; six years earlier during the time I dealt with my back injury.

Within hours of the assault incident, Wendy filed a criminal complaint against me. My heart ached from the accusation.
The news of the filing of charges was presented to Laura and me several days later as Laura returned home from working a Tres Dias retreat weekend.

The emotional impact of those charges in the face of years of being the backup caregiver for her family was catastrophic.
Only God could carry me through that night. Immediately that evening I committed myself to do what God and the law required. I surrendered to the local authorities.

The authorities released me pending the filing of formal charges. I moved out of my home and sought temporary residence in the back of my sister's flower shop.

My next and most important step was to call one of my closest friends, Chuck and ask him to become my accountability partner through this issue. It was not a coincidence, but by God's plan, that Chuck was a leader in the Celebrate Recovery Ministry.

He humbly suggested I might find comfort and relief by beginning a twelve step journey with the help of CR. Without a moment of hesitation, in my brokenness, I attended the next session of CR. That first night I surrendered my control of the outcome of my situation to God's healing power.

I admitted I no longer had the power within myself to manage my life and that in fact, my life had become unmanageable in a continuing cycle of insanity.

I remember vividly the first small group session I attended. To my surprise and comforting, my dear friend Chuck was the ministry leader of that small group for codependency.

I became aware of the concept of codependency years earlier, but without any concrete plan for dealing with my problem, I had no hope of understanding the daily consequences my codependent choices.

I sat listening to Chuck as he read from a small two-page handout. In it, CR described the dynamic of what codependency was. I was stunned as every line of the description fit me perfectly to the letter.

When he was through reading the description portion of the problem I knew for sure I was, in fact, a raging codependent person.

Chuck read on, as the handout also outlined the solution to and recovery from codependency. In just a few minutes, I saw the first glimmer of hope.

I saw that with diligent effort and most importantly the encouraging support of a loving God and Spirit-led ministry team effort I could recover from my addiction to pleasing and placing others needs and burdens above Gods plan for my legitimate needs.

If the evening had ended there, I would have walked away with a tidbit, and probably not continued surrendering my life to God. I didn't know that was just the beginning. In the next hour, I sat and listened to the heart pain and hurts of a room full of brothers in Christ who easily could have been telling my story. The only difference between theirs and mine were the circumstances and situations.

The underlying conflict and their poor ability to cope with the results of fractured male identity were the resonating themes
Finally, I realized the truth that I was in a safe place where I too could begin to verbalize my desperation to do the right thing and therefore be recognized as a good influential man of Godly character.

I walked away seeing how universally wounded we all were with the central issue of discovering and operating out of our true God-given identity as His separately unique child.

For the next year once a week I sat and listened to the reading of that little pamphlet description, and then listened to the hearts of my group brothers.

I would rejoice with them in celebrating the often small but significant victories they described as they made steady slow, careful progress in their recovery. I too was afforded the opportunity to share my victories, and sometimes pains as I progressed as well.

Several months of progress made me ready and hungry for more growth and wisdom. I signed up to take part in the next available step study. The first night 15 brave souls took part in the opening prayers and introduction session.

Each man shared his unique burden and reason to journey through the steps. We all agreed we wanted the opportunity to once and forever rid ourselves of the burdens of carrying the weight of our emotional baggage.

I no longer suffered from the delusion that either my problems or my poor coping skills were a unique affliction. I began to learn what I truly owned as responsibility for my actions.

I could easily admit my powerlessness to make wise choices. There was no reasonable choice but to surrender my life to God's care and control.

As the weeks progressed, I witnessed the steady decline of attendance in the group. Men found all kinds of reasons why they needed to be anywhere but sitting around the discussion table. By the end of the first two months, we were ready to face our first deep challenge.

We were ready to take a fearless spiritual inventory of our lives and work through both the hurts we experienced from others as well as the hurts we had caused.

For some those weeks were an overwhelming obstacle. For me, it was a chance to clean my spiritual house. I carefully chose a sponsor from my brothers and plunged in.

Jeff became one of my most trusted friends over the course of the next several months. He wisely led me through the process. He asked the most pointed and relevant questions helping me probe deeper.

Together we were able to piece together the common threads of cause and effect relationships that tied almost all of my major conflicts together into a common thread of understanding.

We prayed, together, I cried in the midst of the pain of self-discovery. We laughed together; I cried at the capacity to reveal the deepest and darkest secrets locked within my memories.

I grew into wholeness as I was more and more willing to let go and let God heal me from those painful memories.

One evening I was able to share the truth of a yearlong episode of childhood sexual exploitation at the hands of a sexual predator.

Jeff asked me if I could find the strength in my heart to pray God's blessing for that man. At first, I was startled by such a thought, but as I sat there in silence, I was able to have the Holy Spirit minister to me the need to initiate such a prayer.

I began and earnestly asked God to bless him with His forgiveness.

Immediately I felt God's restorative touch and found the cleansing power to express my forgiveness of him as well. I felt an overwhelming burden lifting from my heart as I closed the wound and resulting deep unresolved scar I had carried for over 50 years.

I walked away from that evening session with Jeff and left behind at the throne of God a great load of the baggage I had carried. I knew I was going to be able to leave it all behind in the weeks ahead as I completed my inventory process.

A new and profound peace began to settle into my heart as The Holy Spirit inhabited more and more of the space He had cleansed and restored.

For the first time since facing the turmoil of my criminal circumstances I knew I could find the courage to trust God for all of my needs including the inevitable outcome of those charges. I knew whatever the outcome, God would carry me all the way through, and I had no reason to fear.

I was even ready to accept if necessary a prison sentence if that was what God had for me. I knew God would still find in me a willing vessel to minister to other prisoners in my area of brokenness.

Shortly after my leaving my home, Wendy's entitlement attitude about the possession of Laura's car erupted into another conflict. This time, the eruption was between Wendy and her mother. After several hours of disheartening abusive conflict, Laura insisted that Wendy needed to find another home for herself and her kids.

My heartbroken wife was able to find hope and courage to work through her caught in the middle conflict and asked me to return home. That returning home has been the beginning of a great strengthening of our marriage.

Laura watched as I strived to attend both my step study night and my CR weekly meetings. She was careful to allow me to grow in my fashion. She saw how steadily my life and attitude changed as I found the courage and the strength to lay down forever the hurts resentments and damage of my emotional life.

We began to have a more open and transparent dialogue as I no longer felt the need to hide my true identity behind a wall of fear of her rejection from even the most painful and hurtful moments we still had to deal with in the months ahead.

We became a part of a Tres Dias couples small group that met on Sunday evenings. In that group, we were able to continue the growth of our relationship as we shared our hearts with this group of trusted friends.

As some of you read, I am sure you wonder how we can stay dedicated to so much time in ministry and growth. The reality of our lives is that it is the easiest thing to do with our lives.

Those times are not burdens to be dreaded; they are the lifting of burdens and sharing of burdens of others in intercession to God that enrich our lives and draw us ever closer to the heart of God.

One of the great blessings I received during this process was the provision of a job from my dearest friend Chuck. He owned a 50-year-old terrazzo flooring business in Fort Worth.

Chuck called and recruited me to work in his company as a site supervisor. I knew nothing of the mechanics of the terrazzo business, but I knew Chuck and trusted he would be a great coach where I needed him to be.

I spent seven months steadily working with him on several major projects. The last of those projects was the historic restoration of an ornate terrazzo floor in an old movie theater landmark in Fort Worth. We finished the floor project, but afterward, I was asked to continue the restoration efforts as a contractor.

After years of dwindling resources, God provided me with a new resource that continued to grow in its capacity to provide not only for me but other Christian brothers who were themselves in varying states of their journey of recovery.

I completed the twelve steps and am now a sponsor for another fellow brother on His journey. I know I have grown steadily in my capacity to trust God completely for all of the healing I need in every part of my life.

Not all of us who started the journey made it through to the end. There were only three of us who persevered. I know the Spirit of God will continue to draw those who did not succeed this time through. We say in CR there is no condemnation for failure or relapse. Just keep coming back!

The truth is, our experience of becoming a true believer in the power of God's word spoken intimately and directly into our person is a life long journey. If we still have breath, He has some new and breathtaking revelation of Himself to make. It is His plan for us.

I know there is a season emerging where I will be the willing vessel for Him to use for the strengthening of the lives and faith of others as he weaves us into the fabric of His grand tapestry, His Glorious Church.

I now also celebrate the ending of my criminal case. I chose to accept the opportunity to plead guilty to a misdemeanor offense of unlawful restraint.

It is a part of the irony of my codependent nature that in giving all of my resources to the effort of trying to play God and rescue my family. I spent the vast resource needed to bring my case to a trial for the purpose of receiving a not guilty verdict.

I received a small fine and a sentence of two years adjudicated supervised probation. The fulfillment of that probation obligation is now closed and fulfilled without incident or further consequence.

I do not declare myself blameless in the single incident that occurred ten years ago. I did not solicit Sheyenne to undress, but my insensitive sarcastic remark to her at an difficult and venerable time in my life left her wounded by my course statement.

The nature of my comment offended her and shamed me because it was totally out of the Godly character I strived for in her care. After immediately asking her for her forgiveness, I asked her to keep the incident a secret from others.

I allowed my codependent need to appear perfect in Laura's eyes to prevent me from revealing the incident. I was wrong to do so, and that is in effect an unlawful restraint of Sheyenne's ability to seek help in maintaining her innocent nature at her easily wounded age.

I have no illusion at this time that I am entirely blameless in having a negative effect on her life. I am praying for the day when I can sit in her presence and come to terms of amends for the scar I caused in her life

I also prayed for Sheyenne to find forgiveness of me to help her progress in emerging adult responsibilities. In God's perfect timing that healing has occured.

Over time our family wounds have completely mended. We share holidays and birthdays together without negative words or tension.

Every day I witness the evidence that we are a functioning multigenerational family who genuinely loves and forgives each other. In my entire life experience, that is the most precious gift a person can experience.

I am continuing to remain an active part of the Celebrate Recovery ministry. I know in my heart God has a lot more work for me to do in this vital ministry in God's toolbox of healing and restoration of our broken lives.

Today, however, I celebrate the joy of finishing this book. I celebrate even more the breaking of the chains of bondage that have kept me from being the truly loving Godly man He created me to be.

I had the opportunity to pray for a new understanding of this new found freedom as I prepared to celebrate my completion of my step study. I share with you God's answer to those prayerful days.

I am a Spirit-filled believer walking in freedom

I am FREE....

From the bondage of shame and guilt, that separates me from intimacy with my Creator

From doubt of His powerful presence to help me overcome the faith diminishing effects of life's problems

From the regrets of the past and worries of the future so that I can focus my full attention at the moment

From harmful bias so that I can express and extend loving compassion in all my relationships

From self-absorption so that I can inspire and encourage others as they witness my outward countenance of joy

From fear so that I can experience unshakable inner peace in the midst of the greatest storm.

From bitterness and resentment so that I can respond with kindness even to those who oppose me

From judgmental pride and ruthless arrogance so that I can respond with gentleness to the weak, innocent, and afflicted

From the unbridled desires of the flesh so that I can choose to control self in the face of relentless temptation

Indeed, with God's Mighty hand, I am free to live my life for Him

Epilogue

I first published The Healing Power Of God's Love in March 2013. Sadly, I had little knowledge of the publishing industry or the art of writing. I am gaining both skills after too many years ignoring God's call on my life to make the truth of my testimony known and available.

I am now in my seventieth year of life. I know in my heart, now is the time for the waiting hearts eager to know God better and trust Him completely.

In my original version, I dedicated a large section to discussions of the science underlying my healing experiences. I now feel the prompting of the Lord to simplify things.

I will give you the basic information about of those science experts who shared their research and insights. I hope you have the curiosity after reading my story to look them up and become as convinced as I am about God's masterful craftsmanship in the incredibly complex design of humanity.

I would like to honor and acknowledge Roaring Lambs Ministries for the phenomenal help, writing tools, and the continuing encouragement this now confident writer needed to finish what I started.

Acknowledgements:

I want to acknowledge the scientists and authors who have vastly shaped my thoughts and choices through the process of gaining wisdom and understanding of who God is, and how it is possible to have an intimate personal relationship with Him.

Dr. Charles Lipton:
The Biology of Belief   Dr. Lipton is the research scientist who pioneered the science of epigenetics, a growing field of medical research and practical medical therapy. His book translates the connection between the master craftsmanship of our bodies at the cellular level and its individual awareness of God's presence.

Dr. Caroline Leaf:
Switch on your Brain   World-renowned brain/thought research scientist and public speaker. The developer of 5 step learning process for the capacity to reshape thought process. Dr. Leaf is a staunch advocate and teacher of the relationship between thought process and spiritual awareness through the power of theHoly Spirit.

Heart Math Institute: This scientific research institute began in-depth research of the information processing capability of the heart's nerve center more than 20 years ago. That research clearly outlines the definition of the heart as the information processor for our conscience. This information expanded is priceless in understanding the power of our emotional life.

There is many avenues of learning about God.'s Human craftsmanship. These three authors/researchers are good places to start.

CPSIA information can be obtained
at www.ICGtesting.com
Printed in the USA
LVHW052254250623
750763LV00008B/626

9 781539 096306